# The Way
of
Spiritual Direction

# The Way of Spiritual Direction

*by*

*Francis Kelly Nemeck, O.M.I. and Marie Theresa Coombs, Hermit*

A Michael Glazier Book
THE LITURGICAL PRESS
Collegeville, Minnesota

A Michael Glazier Book published by The Liturgical Press

*Cover design* by David Manahan, O.S.B. Detail of icon of the Holy Trinity by Andrei Rublëv, ca. 1410, Historical Museum, Moscow.

*Imprimi Potest:* Michael Pfeifer, O.M.I., Provincial of the Southern United States Province. *Imprimatur:* Rene H. Gracida, Bishop of Corpus Christi.

| 5 | 6 | 7 | 8 | 9 | 10 | 11 | 12 |
|---|---|---|---|---|---|---|---|

**Library of Congress Cataloging-in-Publication Data**

Nemeck, Francis Kelly, 1936–
    The way of spiritual direction / by Francis Kelly Nemeck and Marie Theresa Coombs.
        p.    cm.
    "A Michael Glazier Book."
    Originally published: Wilmington, Del. : M. Glazier, c1985.
    Includes bibliographical references.
    ISBN 0-8146-5447-9
    1. Spiritual direction.  I. Coombs, Marie Theresa.  II. Title.
BX2350.7.N45   1993
253.5'3—dc20
                                            93-9684
                                          CIP

*To*
*Christ Jesus,*
*the Resurrection and the Life*

"The one who loses his/her life for my sake
will find it" (*Mt* 10:39).

# Table of Contents

# Principal Abbreviations

| | |
|---|---|
| *Ascent* | St. John of the Cross, *The Ascent of Mount Carmel.* |
| *Canticle* | St. John of the Cross, *The Spiritual Canticle* (2nd redaction). |
| *CCSG* | *Corpus Christianorum Series Graeca,* Brepols. |
| *CCSL* | *Corpus Christianorum Series Latina,* Brepols. |
| *Contemplation* | Francis Kelly Nemeck and Marie Theresa Coombs, *Contemplation* (Michael Glazier, Inc., 1723 Delaware Ave., Wilmington, DE 19806) 1982. |
| *C. Prayer* | Thomas Merton, *Contemplative Prayer,* Image D285, 1971. |
| *D. Milieu* | Pierre Teilhard de Chardin, *The Divine Milieu,* Harper TB 384, 1965. |
| *Flame* | St. John of the Cross, *The Living Flame of Love* (2nd redaction). |
| *H. Wisdom* | Augustine Baker, *Holy Wisdom,* Burns and Oates, 1964. |
| *Night* | St. John of the Cross, *The Dark Night of the Soul.* |
| *PG* | *Patrologia Graeca,* Migne. |
| *PL* | *Patrologia Latina,* Migne. |
| *Receptivity* | Francis Kelly Nemeck, *Receptivity* (Van- |

tage Press, Inc., 516 West 34th St., New York, NY 10001) 1984.

*Sayings*        Benedicta Ward, trans., *The Sayings of the Desert Fathers*, Cistercian Publications, 1975.

*S. Direction*   Thomas Merton, *Spiritual Direction and Meditation*, Liturgical Presses, 1960.

*S. Father*      Thomas Merton, "The Spiritual Father in the Desert Tradition," in *Contemplation in a World of Action*, Image D321, 1973.

*Therese*        John Clark, trans., *Story of a Soul: The Autobiography of Therese of Lisieux*, ICS, 1975.

## General Notes

Note 1.  All translations from Hebrew, Greek, Latin, Spanish and French sources are our own. We frequently adapt these texts to express contemporary inclusive language.

Note 2.  While one may quite legitimately speak of the motherhood of God, we use "fatherhood" throughout this study in reference to God since this word approximates more closely biblical terminology. Furthermore, the biblical notion of the fatherhood of God incorporates and completely transcends everything that could possibly comprise human fatherhood and motherhood.

Note 3.  Following the Western mystical tradition, we use the word "soul" in this study synonymously with "person." We thus designate the deepest and most mysterious aspects of the human person being acted upon by God. This usage does not come from the scholastic *corpus-anima* distinction, but rather is derived from the Hebrew *nephesh* and from the New Testament *psyche*.

# Introduction

All great spiritual writers and founders of religious orders have insisted on the need to have a spiritual director. No novice or seminarian has ever gotten through formation without one (or two, or three). Everyone needs a guide, a confidant, a friend at one time or another. Most people can benefit from a psychologist or a counselor, professional or otherwise, at the more decisive moments of life. We all need someone special at certain times. God never fails to provide the right person in the right context, although we do not necessarily recognize that gift as such.

The various ways of fostering emotional, psychological and spiritual growth within an individual dialogue with each other and contribute to the deeper integration of the human person. Yet, of all the possible ways of assisting a person mature the most difficult and also the most neglected is undoubtedly spiritual direction. We mean *real* spiritual direction.

It is a sign of our times that more people than ever are seeking spiritual guidance. Yet, experience has proven that most are hard pressed to find it in any meaningful depth. The very persons whom one would expect to be qualified spiritual directors are too often found either woefully reluctant to accept the responsibility or downright incompetent: one's pastor, a priest or religious acquaintance, the professors of theology at the nearest college or university, the

13

trained chaplains in the local hospital or hospice, and above all retreat masters, formation directors and major superiors.

Some insightful material on the practice of spiritual direction has been produced in recent years by such writers as Jean Laplace, Adrian van Kaam and Kenneth Leech. Yet, none of these authors explores in sufficient depth the theology of spiritual guidance. What is especially lacking in our day is a thorough treatment of the contemplative dimension inherent in all spiritual direction.

We are not referring so much to the spiritual guidance of contemplatives as such, but rather to the direction of the contemplative element found within all who seek interior progress regardless of lifestyle or vocation. We mean the contemplative thrust integral to the universal call to holiness.[1] In this respect, both St. John of the Cross (1542-1591) and Thomas Merton (1915-1968) excel. Nonetheless, their writings pose considerable difficulty for the uninitiated reader. Their teachings on the theology, contemplative dimension and dynamics of spiritual direction are scattered piecemeal throughout their works.

Our study gleans insights from scripture, from the mystical tradition of the Church and specifically from these two spiritual masters. We then build on these insights and adapt them to contemporary needs. Thus, we present a workable synthesis for the serious pilgrim on life's interior journey.

Our book is neither a compendium nor a textbook. Rather, it constitutes a comprehensive study of the mystery and dynamics of the contemplative dimension inherent to all spiritual direction for any person in any walk of life.

---

[1]See *Contemplation*, pp. 13-20.

## Chapter 1

# Spiritual Regeneration

One of the first questions which a young child preparing for first Communion is taught to pose is this: Why did God make me? Undoubtedly, one of the most soul-searching questions any adult must sooner or later ask is this: Why am I?

The theological response to both these questions is the same: Each of us has been brought into being out of the superabundance of God's love, and we are each called to transforming union in him. To put it more biblically: We are to return to the Father with his Son in the Holy Spirit.

The Son proceeds from the Father from all eternity and is begotten by him in time. The only begotten Son, Christ Jesus, is God's Word made flesh (*Jn* 1:14). Jesus returns resurrected to the Father. This is the passover of the Lord.

The human person is created by God and is destined to "become God by participation."[1] Together with Jesus and through him, we return to the Father in the Spirit. This is our passover in the Lord.

This process, this return journey, may be called spiritual regeneration (after the manner of *Jn* 3 and 4); deification, divinization or christification (in the sense of 1 *Co* 15:28 or

---

[1] *Ascent* II, 5, 7. See *Contemplation*, pp. 16-18.

*Col* 3:11); transformation in Christ, in God (as per 2 *Co* 3:18); spiritualization (following *Rm* 8, 1 *Co* 2 and 15); interiorization (in the sense of 2 *Co* 4:16); sanctification (according to 1 *Th* 4:3).

Spiritual direction then is the gift, the charism, the ministry of guiding a person in and through his/her passover in the Lord. It is a unique participation in another's spiritual regeneration, deification, transformation. Spiritual direction is a God-willed contribution of one person to another's process of spiritualization, interiorization, sanctification.

Let us examine more closely some of the theological presuppositions of these truths.

## A. Eternal Generation-Spiration

### (1) THE FATHER AND THE SON

According to the Hebrew scriptures, God let himself be experienced initially as the God of our fathers (i.e., of Abraham, Isaac, Jacob: *Ex* 3:6). Later, around the time of the exile, Israel became conscious of God as "our Father" (*Is* 63:16) and even as "my Father" (*Jr* 3:19).

It is only with the advent of Christ, however, that the full import of God *the* Father is appreciated. Yet, Jesus himself never speaks of the Father as *our* Father. (In Matthew's version of the Lord's prayer *Mt* 6:9 —the word "our" is probably an addition by the primitive Church used in reference to its membership as a whole.) Rather, Jesus consistently distinguishes "my Father" from "your Father" as in *Jn* 20:17. There is of course no difference in the Father as such. But there is a world of difference between Jesus's relationship to his Father and our relationship to his Father.

At the time of Christ every devout Jew believed that s/he was a son or daughter of God. But Jesus revealed himself as the only begotten Son of the Father. This truth did not escape the attention of his adversaries either: "The Jews became even more intent on killing him. Not only did he break the sabbath, but he spoke of God as his own Father, and so made himself God's equal" (*Jn* 5:18).

St. Augustine captures the sense of this mystery very succinctly: "It is one thing to be taught to honor God as God. It is quite another to approach him as the Father. When you honor him as God, it is as Creator, as Almighty, as Spirit. But when you approach him as the Father, you are also honoring his Son."[2]

The mystery of the person of Jesus, together with our incorporation in him, cannot possibly be understood except in direct reference to the Father: his Father and ours. We are, therefore, sons and daughters in the Son.

## (2) THE FATHER AND THE SON: COEXISTENT FROM ALL ETERNITY

"In the beginning, the Word already existed. The Word was with God. Indeed, the Word was God" (*Jn* 1:1).

These incomparable lines of the beloved disciple constitute the beginning of all theological discourse on the mystery of the Trinity.

The person of the Son and the person of the Father are coequally God in such a way that the one proceeds eternally from the other. As the Father is without age, so the Son is without growth or subordination. Equal generates equal. Eternal begets eternal. This is like a flame generating light. The flame remains distinct from the light which proceeds from it. Yet, the generating flame does not precede the generated light. They are coequal, coexistent as the one proceeds distinctly from the other. "Show me a flame without light, and I will show you God the Father without the Son."[3]

[2] Commentary on *Jn* 5:19-30 (*CCSL*, 36, 190-191. *PL*, 35:1546).

[3] St. Augustine, Commentary on *Jn* 5:19 (*CCSL*, 36, 207-208. *PL*, 35:1560).

## (3)THE FATHER AND THE SON AS ONE

"The Father is in me and I am in the Father." Indeed, "the Father and I are one" (*Jn* 10:30, 38). This union is abiding. It is eternal. Furthermore, this union is communion.

The word "union" means joined together, united. "Communion," on the other hand, accentuates the personal, loving, intimate being-one-with-the-other. "You are my beloved Son" (*Mk* 1:11). "The Father loves the Son" (*Jn* 3:35). Moreover, Jesus was personally conscious of his loving communion with the Father: "I abide in his love" (*Jn* 15:10).

Jesus reveals something of the intimacy of this loving interchange in the title *abba: Abba*, "Father, holy is your name" (*Lk* 11:2). "*Abba*, Father, take this cup from me" (*Mk* 14:36).

The Aramaic *abba* derives from the Hebrew *abh* and was originally spoken by small children as a familiar and endearing way to address their fathers: hence, "daddy." At the time of Jesus, *abba* was also used in intimate conversation with one's "dad." So familiar was this term that no Jew dared use it in relation to God.

St. Paul readily caught the nuances of this logion of the Lord and applied it to the interior life of the Christian: "You have received the Spirit who makes you sons and daughters. By him we cry: *Abba*, Father" (*Rm* 8:15). "God sent the Spirit of his Son into our hearts crying: *Abba*, Father" (*Ga* 4:6).

The intimacy between the Father and the Son is expressed sometimes by the Greek verb *horao* (to see, to behold, to be admitted into the more immediate presence of): "No one has seen the Father except the one who is from God. He has seen the Father" (*Jn* 6:46). "Whoever has seen me has seen the Father" (*Jn* 14:9). *Horao* in this context means to contemplate the Other in an immediate and direct way. It is to encounter in love that which is deepest and most intimate in the Other: the other's person. Thus, the Father and the Son contemplate one another, so that all who contemplate the One share by participation in the contemplation of the

Other. For the Father is in the Son, just as the Son is in the Father (*Jn* 14:10).

Elsewhere the verb *ginosko* (to know, to experience) accentuates the immediacy of the love between Jesus and his *abba*: "The Father knows me, and I know the Father" (*Jn* 10:15). Moreover, "no one knows who the Son is except the Father, just as no one knows the Father except the Son" (*Lk* 10:22). This is obviously not so much knowledge of or about one another, as it is direct and intuitive communion in love, the One abiding in the Other. This loving interchange Jesus shares with "whomever he wills" (*Mt* 11:27).

So profound is this intimate communion that everything the Father does or has or is, is shared with his Son: "The Father loves the Son and shows him all that he himself does" (*Jn* 5:20), because "everything my Father has is mine" (*Jn* 16:15). The Father and the Son act together, yet distinctly, in everything: "The Son cannot of himself do anything unless he sees the Father doing it" (*Jn* 5:19).

## (4) THE FATHER, THE SON AND THE SPIRIT

"God is Spirit" (*Jn* 4:24). "God is love" (1 *Jn* 4:16).

The coequal Son proceeds from the Father from all eternity. This is called divine generation. The coequal Spirit proceeds from the Father and the Son from all eternity. This is called divine spiration. As St. Augustine puts it: "The Holy Spirit is he whereby the begotten Son is loved by the begetting Father and loves his Begetter."[4] Indeed the loving communion between the Father and the Son is so intimately personal that together they spirate the person of the Holy Spirit.[5]

In scholastic theology, the verb "spirate" adds a particular quality to the notion "love." Spirate denotes the conscious endorsement of one's love, which leads to a permanent union between lover and beloved.

---

[4] *The Trinity*, 6, 5, 7 (*CCSL*, 50, 235. *PL*, 42:928).
[5] See St. Thomas Aquinas, *Sum. Theo.*, I, 36-37.

To extend St. Augustine's analogy of the flame and its light mentioned above, not only does light proceed from the flame, but warmth also proceeds from the flame and the light. The warmth is distinct from the flame and the light, yet coexistent with them. Neither the flame nor the light nor the warmth precedes one another. They are concomitant. We cannot be shown a flame without light and warmth.

God is Father, Son and Spirit. Each is coequal, coexistent, co-eternal with the others.

## B. *Our Return to the Father with the Son in the Spirit*

The loving communion between the persons of the Trinity is diffusive: that is, it tends by its very nature to radiate out from its center. One of the most concrete manifestations for us of this divine, loving diffusiveness is our own individual creation.

God does not create us because he sees that we are good. His creation of us makes us good, lovable. His act of creation precedes any lovableness on our part. We come into being solely out of God's infinite, superabundant love. His love creates us lovable. Thus, each human person is born, generated into this life.

God is not content to create us merely "good" (*Gn* 1:25), however. He makes us "very good" (*Gn* 1:31), after his own image and likeness (*Gn* 1:27). God creates the human person as destined to transforming union in him. Thus, we are called to be re-born, re-generated to eternal life.

In this manner, we speak of our return to the Father with the Son in the Spirit. Obviously the word "return" cannot be said of us in the same way that it applies to Christ. The eternal Word preexisted his incarnation. The eternal person of the Son is identical with the person of Jesus who was conceived, was born and died at a particular time and place. In actual fact, none of us preexisted our earthly existence. In an analogous sense, however, we have been "foreknown and predestined" (*Rm* 8:29) in the eternal love of the Father, Son and Spirit. Thus, our "return" is not to where we actually were before, but rather to the fullness of the loving goodness to which God's love calls us. In this fullness God becomes all in us (1 *Co* 15:28); Christ becomes all in us (*Col* 3:11).

Love by its very nature is diffusive and unitive. Diffusiveness connotes the act of generation: one proceeding from another. Union denotes movement towards a center: a kind of return. In our regard, God's love is at the same time creative (we are brought into being out of nothing), generative (we are made his children), and unitive (we are called to attain our fullness of being only in him). Yet, this fullness is infinitely beyond anything we could ever achieve of ourselves (1 *Co* 2:9). By reason of the utter transcendency of our ultimate destiny in God, his love for us is not only creative, but re-creative (2 *Co* 5:17); not just generative, but regenerative (*Jn* 3:3); not merely unitive in some vague sense, but re-unitive with him in transforming union: "We are being transformed into the Lord's likeness with ever increasing glory" (2 *Co* 3:18).

Thus, the human person is transformed in God: "lover transformed in Beloved."⁶ We become divinized, deified. "God so communicates his supernatural being to the soul that it seems to be God himself, possessing whatever God has." Moreover, "so perfect is this union that everything both of God and of the soul is one in participant transformation." In this manner, "the soul seems more God than soul. Indeed, it is God by participation."⁷

We do not say, however, that the human person is transformed *into* God, since this phrase could suggest an absorption into God which would cause the loss of individual personality. On the contrary, our deification brings the uniqueness of our personhood to ultimate fulfillment in such a way that God remains God and we remain ourselves, but transformed in God.

The Father, the Son and the Spirit remain uniquely distinct, yet united as one God. Transformed in God, we

---

⁶*Amada en el Amado transformada*, poem by St. John of the Cross: *En una noche oscura*, stanza 5.

⁷*Ascent*, II, 5, 7. See *Contemplation*, pp. 16-18.

remain creatures personally distinct from the Trinity and from each other while being God by participation. The communion of the divine persons constitutes the Trinity. Our communion in God with Father, Son and Spirit constitutes transforming union: heaven, beatitude, eternal life.

In spiritual direction, God gifts one human being with the grace to assist another in achieving a greater voluntary cooperation with God's own transforming activity within that other.

The phrase "transforming union" designates both the goal and the whole process from beginning to end. The phrase "spiritual regeneration" means the same (i.e., both the goal and the way). However, spiritual regeneration accentuates the activity of the Son and of the Spirit in our return to the Father.

Spiritual regeneration comes about this way: The Son being God —coequal and coeternal with the Father and the Spirit — did not consider this something to be clung to, but emptied himself by becoming a servant (*Ph* 2:6-7). The eternal Word became human just like each of us, but without sin (*Heb* 4:15). Jesus so humbled himself that he became obedient unto death, death on a cross. Whereupon, God resurrected him (*Ph* 2:8-11).

The integral mystery of the Passover of the Lord consists of Jesus's incarnation, death and resurrection. By his incarnation the eternal Word became flesh (*Jn* 1:14). But his humanity could not reach the full stature of its development until his personal death. Just like each of us, Jesus was not fully human except in death, even though he was truly human and divine from the first moment of his earthly existence. Furthermore, Christ's resurrection did not so much follow upon his death in the sense of coming after it, as we perceive these events in time; rather Jesus's resurrection occurred especially in his death, through it and out of it. Thus, the Son's coming forth from the Father, together with his return, is in reality one continuous movement of which God is the source, the way and the goal. The movement itself comprises a series of thresholds in time. It takes place by way of kenosis: emptying (*Ph* 2:7).

As a matter of historical fact, the only way that God has become human so that we can be divinized is by way of kenosis. The Son emptied himself, taking on a human nature in such a way that his humanity was gradually transformed by his divinity. This transformation reached its ultimate threshold in Jesus's death out of which he rose totally God and totally human.

Similarly for us. As a matter of historical fact, there is only one way we can return to our Father. That way is with his Son, our Brother and our Lord, by way of kenosis. We must enter into his kenosis, his death-resurrection (*Rm* 6:3-4). This is what is lacking in the sufferings of Christ (*Col* 1:24): our voluntary cooperation and incorporation. We simply were not there at the time of his passover. However, there exists an important difference between Jesus's kenosis and ours. Christ emptied himself. We *are emptied* by him of everything in us that is not transformable in God.[8]

## C. Freedom of the Children of God

The eternal Word is the Father's Son by essence. We are sons and daughters in the Son by adoption and participation (*Eph* 1:5). Because we are his adopted children, God has sent the Spirit of his Son into our hearts so that we too may pray: *Abba*, Father (*Ga* 4:5-6; *Rm* 8:15). This adoption, or spiritual regeneration, is a veritable birthing process, the birth pangs of which constitute a major portion of our kenosis (*Rm* 8:18-23). The firstfruit, as it were, of this kenosis is freedom, "freedom of the children of God" (*Rm* 8:21).

We may choose between good and evil. We may opt for one of several alternatives. But we are truly free only in relation to the greatest good. The ability in this life to choose a lesser good, or even evil, is an abuse of freedom. It is non-freedom: slavery to sin (*Rm* 7:14).

[8]See *Contemplation*, pp. 34-35.

Christ himself is our freedom, since he is our truth (*Jn* 14:6). And the truth has set us free (*Jn* 8:32). "If, therefore, the Son makes you free, you will be free indeed" (*Jn* 8:36). Learning this truth and being set free by it is literally a lifelong process, coextensive with our transformation and kenosis.

The ultimate threshold of all this spiritual regeneration is death. For many persons, if not most, however, a significant threshold in this process is reached well before death. This experience carries different names in diverse circumstances: "born again," "conversion," "fundamental option," "baptism in the Spirit." What is common to all these expressions of basically the same soul-rending experience is the consciousness of and the explicit cooperation with the freedom to grow more directly in Christ. Even though sin continues to live in me (*Rm* 7:14-25), I can still affirm with increasing awareness that as I become "crucified with Christ, I live now, no longer I, but Christ lives in me" (*Ga* 2:19-20).

From the inception of this threshold of interior regeneration, the ministry of spiritual direction assumes increasing significance. Spiritual direction helps directees quicken the awareness of their deeper freedom as children of God as well as their responsibility to live their call worthily (*Eph* 4:1). Spiritual direction helps explicate whatever particulars directees may need to know regarding their return to the Father. Spiritual direction is a special means which the Father uses to awaken directees to the consciousness of the regeneration of his Son within them and to the engendering of his Spirit all around them (*Ps* 104:30)

## Chapter 2

# Spiritualization-Interiorization

In the preceding chapter on spiritual regeneration we dealt principally with the notion of regeneration. In the present chapter we shall consider more directly the notion of spiritual. Our rebirth is not in just any direction. We are reborn solely in the direction of spirit (*Jn* 3:5).

## A. Spiritual: pneumatikos

The New Testament word *pneumatikos*, which we translate "spiritual," refers to whatever pertains to the Spirit or is influenced by the Spirit. The term itself is found almost exclusively in St. Paul. Its meaning is more properly grasped when viewed in relation to its opposites. Paul contrasts "spiritual" to "fleshy" (in *Romans*) and to "natural" (in 1 *Corinthians*).

In the opening statement of the confession of his interior struggle, Paul describes his own personal situation as well as that of humankind: "The law as we all know is spiritual, but I am fleshy (*sarkinos*)" (*Rm* 7:14). Paul consistently distinguishes *sarx* (flesh) from *soma* (body). *Soma* connotes the human person, stressing our exterior and behavioral dimensions. The complement of *soma* is *psyche* (soul) which connotes the same human person, but stresses our more interior and imperceptible aspects. *Sarx,* on the other hand, is usually for Paul flesh in the fleshiest sense: sinful, sinning, sinner.

"The law as we all know is spiritual." Paul uses the word "law" over sixty times in *Romans* alone. Moreover, he gives the term a myriad of nuances. In all likelihood "law" in *Rm* 7:14 refers to "the law of the Spirit of life in Christ Jesus" (*Rm* 8:2). This of course is spiritual. It derives from the Spirit living in us, and it is developing towards more intense spiritualization of both the interior as well as exterior dimensions of the human person.

Yet, Paul does not state specifically what spiritualization consists of. Without doubt, the reason for this is that the eye has not seen, the ear has not heard, it has not so much as entered into the imagination of anyone what spiritual means concretely in all its fullness (1 *Co* 2:9). However, we all know from personal experience the meaning of "fleshy." And spiritual is the opposite of *sarx.*

In the context of the mystery of the resurrection, Paul again contrasts spiritual, but this time not so much with *fleshy* as with *soma psychikon*: "a natural body" (1 *Co* 15:44). *Soma* may be translated by "body" in the holistic sense described above. But *psychikon* (literally: breathing, sensate) is very difficult to render. Many translators settle for "natural" since Paul is obviously referring to the human person in this natural, mortal life: the life into which we are born. The resurrected life of the "spiritual body" (*soma pneumatikon*) is the complete transformation of what we now experience in this present life. It is our definitive rebirth.

There is, however, an important difference in these two contrasts by Paul. Spiritual is as diametrically opposed to fleshy as godliness is to sinfulness. Spiritual is also opposed to natural, but not necessarily in a pejorative sense, as if there is something innately wrong with being natural. Rather, natural is of itself incapable of spiritual. The Spirit transforms the natural into the spiritual, leaving behind whatever is fleshy and untransformable.

Spiritual, therefore, designates that towards which we are all being moved. It is that into which we are being transformed. The agent of this process is God himself: the Holy Spirit. We are already becoming spiritual. But we are not yet completely spiritual (*Rm* 8:24-25), for this side of death we are still fleshy and we are still in our *soma psychikon*. However, God is inexorably bringing to completion what he has begun (*Ph* 1:6).

Thus, when we use the term "spiritual direction," we do mean *spiritual* direction.

## B. The Spiritual Direction of Creation

Properly understood, *Rm* 8:22-23 and *Col* 1:15-20 testify to the fact that all creation is in tension. It is developing. God is moving all creation in an increasingly spiritual direction.

To paraphrase Pierre Teilhard de Chardin, matter is becoming spirit.[1] Spirit is that which matter is becoming in much the same way that St. Paul speaks of our "natural bodies" becoming "spiritual" in the resurrection (1 *Co* 15:44).

God brings all creation and each individual creature into being in such a way that that created being must *become* what it is meant to be. To create means to bring into being becoming. Evolution then is God's process of creating.

Two graphic symbols help us picture this overall development: the inverted cone and the ascending-converging spi-

---

[1]See, for example: *The Heart of the Matter* (Harcourt, 1978), pp. 25-29, 90-102; *The Phenomenon of Man* (Harper, 1959); *Activation of Energy* (Harcourt, 1971), pp. 21-57, 141-151; *The Future of Man* (Torchbooks, 1964), pp. 85-100.

ral. (In each representation "X" stands for Christ, and "c" represents creation at its inception.)

*The cone*          *The spiral*

X                   X

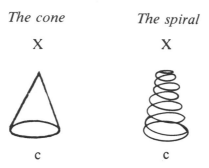

c                   c

Christ is the Alpha and the Omega, the beginning and the end (*Rv* 22:13). He is the firstborn (i.e., the first to be completely reborn) and the head of all creation (*Col* 1:15, 18). In him, through him, for him were created all things in heaven and on earth (*Col* 1:16, 19). He holds all things together, for in him resides the fullness of everything and everyone (*Col* 1:17, 19).

God creates being becoming. The symbol of the cone accentuates the fact that all creation is brought into being in a scattered, disjointed, imperfect state of being. Therefore, it must become, evolve, develop into what it is fully meant to be. As this development takes place "c" is transformed in "X", yet with persistence of "c" in "X". To apply this principle to the human condition in the resurrection: We are transformed in Christ, in God, in such a way that something of everything in our individual lives endures, yet without the modalities of this "natural" existence.

The image of the spiral adds the note of sequential thresholds to the symbol of the cone. The ultimate threshold in our individual lives is death. For humanity as a whole that threshold is the parousia. Between conception and resurrection, between the beginning and the end, there are many significant thresholds or passages, all dialoguing one with the other, all converging towards our ultimate breakthrough. This whole process, whether individual or collective, consists in spiritualization. It is towards spirit.

There exist two contradictory, all-pervasive forces within creation: entropy and evolution.

Entropy turns creation in upon itself and tries to reverse its spiritual development. Entropy is innately "fleshy." It is regression into matter, scatteredness, the multiple. In the human sphere, entropy is selfishness, self-centeredness, the sin of the world (*Jn* 1:29).

Evolution, on the other hand, is specifically the aspect of becoming within creation. It is from God and to him. God's creative activity is the very core of evolution. In the human sphere this energy is none other than love, the gift of self.

Theoretically at least, evolution could proceed in a variety of possible directions. As a matter of fact, however, there is only one direction of evolution: towards the point of ultimate consummation — Christ, Omega. Thus, evolution is in genesis (from the Greek *ginomai*: to become). The Word *became* flesh and bestowed upon us the power to *become* children of God (*Jn* 1:14, 12), so that in him we *become* a new creation (2 *Co* 5:17).

In more technical terminology, we say that the evolution of the world — cosmogenesis — is in fact Christogenesis. For Christ himself, God, is becoming "all in all" (*Col* 3:11; 1 *Co* 15:28). And since God is Spirit (*Jn* 4:24), we are becoming spirit, spiritual, spirified (1 *Co* 15:44). Because of Christ, therefore, evolution has only one direction: spiritual.

Evolution, or genesis, proceeds by way of a dialectical process. Each threshold in our personal lives as well as each threshold of evolution as a whole comprises three elements: divergence, convergence, emergence. Divergence is the expression of the inner need within genesis to search out in every possible direction those avenues which are compatible with our becoming properly the persons we are called to become. After certain experiences, however, we realize through a process of elimination that only certain avenues are in fact compatible with our development. Things begin to converge. Finally, these converging avenues reach such an intensity of concentration that we emerge through a threshold to a more mature and interiorized state of being than previously existed. At this point, the dialectic begins all over again, but always towards heightened being becoming.

An example of this process is the teenager who in the context of dating first plays the field. After a while s/he begins dating only a certain type of person. Sooner or later, a commitment to one person emerges which is expressed first in going steady, then in engagement and finally in marriage.

In every threshold there are both continuity and discontinuity. In passing into adulthood, we leave behind the ways of childhood and of adolescence (1 *Co* 13:11-12). Yet, we are always the same persons progressing through the successive thresholds becoming more and more our true selves. At each new emergence, we are more spiritualized, more transformed, more interiorized. The real God (as opposed to the god of our imagination or feelings) is encountered more deeply and more directly within ourselves as well as more extensively and more immediately in the totality of creation.

Matter is the matrix of spirit.[2] Matter for each of us is that complex of energies, influences, persons and things which surround us inasmuch as they are palpable, sensible and "natural." Matter is the concrete milieu in which our becoming is effected and affected.

As such, matter has two faces. On the one hand, it burdens. It fetters. Matter is a prime source of pain and sin. It weighs us down. It wounds us, tempts us, makes us grow old. Who will deliver us from this body doomed to death (*Rm* 7:24)? But on the other hand, matter is physical exuberance, ennobling contact, virile effort, the joy of growth. It attracts, renews, unites, blossoms. In matter we live and move and have our being (*Acts* 17:28). Who will bestow on us this spiritual body (1 *Co* 15:44)?

---

[2]See, for instance: Teilhard de Chardin, *D. Milieu*, pp. 105-111; *The Heart of Matter* (Harcourt, 1978), pp. 225-229; *Human Energy* (Harcourt, 1969), pp. 19-47, 93-112; *Christianity and Evolution* (Harcourt, 1971), pp. 138-150, 237-243.

Matter can be likened to the mountain up whose slope a climber scales. At any given point along the way, space is divided into two zones: the summit which lies up ahead and the abyss below. Only the person moves up or down. Matter provides the support for the movement.[3] The person is drawn irresistibly toward the goal, regardless of obstacles or difficulties.

Thus, matter for each of us has two conflicting meanings: the burden of flesh and the matrix of spirit. Matter is the womb out of which spirit evolves. Matter does not produce spirit. Only *the* Spirit can cause spiritualization. But it is produced out of matter, not just in the sense that a glass holds the water which is poured from it, but rather in the sense that matter itself is transformed by the Spirit into spirit. Spirit is the spiritual form of matter. Thus, spiritualization is not anti-matter, or extra-matter, but trans-matter.[3]

The spiritual director, therefore, helps bring into consciousness and explicate the already existing spiritual direction in which the Spirit is leading the directee.


## C. Interiorization

The spiritual life is an interior life. "The kingdom of God is within you" (*Lk* 17:21). Spiritualization is accomplished by interiorization: "Though outwardly we are wasting away, inwardly we are being renewed day by day" (2 *Co* 4:16).

Interiorization may be seen as a particular modality of the process of spiritualization. The interior quality of life denotes letting God who dwells within us draw us ever deeper into himself. God is everywhere. But we can never encounter the real God outside ourselves until we first discover him deep within our own being. This truth is analogous to the fact that we can never truly love another person until we are able to love ourselves.

[3]See *Receptivity*, pp. 109-120.

We are born into this world. But we are reborn spiritually only by passing all the way through ourselves and through this world. Spiritual regeneration is accomplished not by withdrawal from the world: from persons, from situations or from things. Rather, it is accomplished by becoming incarnate and involved all the way through the world to God. Jesus became incarnate unto death inclusive (*Ph* 2:7-8).[4]

Thus, spiritual direction deals with the interior life of directees: their life in God, and in him their life with all creation. Spiritual direction addresses the process of interiorization in such a way as to awaken directees to a consciousness of the path along which God is leading them. They in turn can then more voluntarily cooperate with God as he draws them through the passages of life.

Yet, the responsibility of a spiritual director is not specifically to give a spiritual direction to the directee. No, "your work is that of preparing the soul. It is God's work to direct its way to spiritual blessings by ways and in manners that neither you nor the soul can understand."[5]

[4]See *Receptivity*, pp. 17-53, 114-120.

[5]*Flame*, 3, 47. John is referring to *Pr* 16:1 and 9.

*Chapter 3*

# The Spiritual Director as *Abba/Amma*

The fatherhood of God is the pivot upon which hinges the mystery of the Trinity. The paternity of God is also the beginning of all theological discourse on the mystery of our adoption as his children in his Son. The Father generates the Son. The Father and the Son together spirate in love the Holy Spirit, who in turn regenerates us with the very life of God. This is our passover in the Lord. Thus, the Father together with the Son and the Spirit is the source and the goal of all life, both "natural" and "spiritual" (1 *Co* 15:44).

In revealing God not only as Father, but specifically as *the* Father and *his* Father (*Jn* 5:18), Jesus insists that no true father/motherhood can exist apart from the *one* Father: "You have only one father, and he is in heaven" (*Mt* 23:9). Paul puts the same truth in other words: "There is only one God who is Father of all, over all, through all, within all" (*Eph* 4:6). It is from him alone that "all fatherhood" and motherhood "whether in heaven or on earth takes its name" (*Eph* 3:15).

In the case of natural birth, God uses natural parenthood to generate life. Through their mutual love a man and a woman engender and nurture another human being. Yet, the life to which they give birth is itself a gift they receive from a source beyond themselves. They transmit this life to another. Our parents prepare the matter out of which God himself brings forth a person.

As in natural birth, so in spiritual rebirth. As the Father uses natural parenthood to engender natural life, so our Father uses spiritual father/motherhood to engender new life in the Spirit. Spiritual parenthood is thus a charismatic participation in the very fatherhood of God. The early Church took very seriously the logion of Jesus: "Call no one on earth your father, for you have only one Father, and he is in heaven" (*Mt* 23:9). The desert fathers and mothers were so termed precisely because they participated in such a unique and God-willed manner in the parenthood of the Father.

A spiritual father or mother is one called to be, either for a brief or an extended time, a special instrument in the spiritual regeneration of others. S/he participates in the regenerating, recreative work of God by awakening and quickening in others the life of the Spirit. Under the guidance of the Spirit, s/he helps them discern their spiritual direction. Furthermore, through the person of the spiritual father or mother the Father allows directees to experience something of his own tender, compassionate, unfathomable love.

God may call one to exercise spiritual paternity/maternity through a variety of ways: as pastor, counselor, teacher, nurse, friend, mother, father, brother, sister, husband, wife. Every Christian vocation implies to some extent a call to help spiritually those to whom one is sent. One very unique expression of spiritual parenthood, however, is the ministry which has come to be termed "spiritual direction."

This charism has its roots in scripture, particularly in the letters of Paul and John. Paul enumerates essential qualities of this gift in some of his lists of the *charismata*: prophecy, teaching, encouragement, sharing in simplicity (*Rm* 12:6-8); shepherding (*Eph* 4:11); interior healing, discernment (1 *Co* 12:30). In his own pastoral attitude towards specific persons, Paul further testifies to his spiritual paternity: for example, by addressing Titus as his "child" in the faith they share together (*Tt* 1:4). To the Christian community at Corinth, Paul proclaims "In Christ Jesus I became your father" (1 *Co* 4:15). Elsewhere he makes reference to his spiritual maternity: "My dear children, I go through the pain of giving rebirth to you until Christ is formed in you" (*Ga* 4:19). He compares himself in another text to "a mother caring for her children" (1 *Th* 2:7). The beloved disciple also bears witness to this gift as he in turn addresses the Christian community which he helped engender spiritually: "my dear children" (1 *Jn* 2:1).

Nonetheless, what we call today "spiritual direction" comes into full bloom with the onset of monasticism and the eremitical movement in the Middle East. Countless persons began spontaneously to seek out spiritual guidance from the desert fathers and mothers: the *abbas* and *ammas*.

Three particular characteristics of the desert fathers and mothers exemplify qualities intrinsic to a true spiritual director: (A) They were solitaries, persons of prayer, men and women of God. (B) They were spiritual persons. (C) They found themselves sought out by others for spiritual guidance.

## (A) Solitaries: Persons of Prayer

Not everyone who has ever gone out into the desert is necessarily a spiritual father or mother. Plenty of bandits, iconoclasts, bedouin still roam the wilderness. The abbas and ammas of the fourth, fifth and sixth centuries, however, were sincere men and women who sought out God in a very particular way in the deserts of Palestine, Syria and Egypt. In a real sense they were anarchists for the sake of Chirst (*Mk* 10:29). Refusing to let themselves be swept along passively by a decadent state, they believed and demonstrated that there was a way of living without slavish dependence on conventional values — values which were far from the Gospel. As the letter to the Hebrews (11:37-38) refers to their Jewish counterparts, so were these Christian abbas and ammas: "They went about in sheepskins and in the hides of goats; homeless, persecuted and misunderstood. Society was not worthy of them. Therefore, they went out to live in deserts and on mountains, in caves and near ravines."

Yet, they did not arrogantly reject society or human companionship. Rather they were in quest of a society where they could become their true selves in Christ. "They sought a way to God that was uncharted and freely chosen, not inherited from others who had mapped it out beforehand. They sought a God whom they alone could find, not one who was 'given' in a set, stereotyped form by somebody else."[1] The desert fathers and mothers were not running away from anything. They were not shirking responsibility. They were not withdrawing from society. On the contrary, they were drawn inexorably into solitude. They were impelled by the Gospel and by God to get in touch more directly with the soul-searching questions of life, death and eternity.

The desert represented for the abbas and ammas infinitely more than mere external solitude. Exterior solitude was the milieu in which they each undertook the more difficult and hazardous journey through the desert of the heart. The rugged emptiness of the desert was the place of intimate, loving communion with God. In the light of the incomprehensible love and mercy of their Father, they faced the naked truth of themselves.

As the love of God gradually stripped them of their false, illusory selves, they began to experience their transformed selves emerge slowly, yet ever more strongly. By growing in the hidden life of Jesus, the love, peace and joy of Christ became increasingly transparent in them.

Like the abbas and ammas, the spiritual director must also have personal experience of the desert: specifically, the desert of the heart.

The basis of any authentic prayer life is interpersonal, loving communion with the indwelling Father, Son and Spirit. To be persons of prayer we must above all seek God

---

[1]Thomas Merton, *The Wisdom of the Desert* (New Directions, 1960), p. 6.

within ourselves in faith and love. "The Word, the Son of God, together with the Father and the Holy Spirit, is hidden in essence and in presence in the innermost being of the soul. A person who desires to find God must be detached from all things, and enter within him/herself in deepest recollection."[2]

In order to pass beyond self and enter into direct communion with God, solitude of heart is essential. This quality enables us to remain always in loving interchange with God whether we are actually alone or in a crowd, whether in prayer or in activity, whether at work or at recreation.

To foster interior solitude, some exterior solitude is necessary. How much physical solitude may be required can be determined by certain principles.[3] Like Jesus, we need to go off to some place where we can actually be alone and pray (*Lk* 5:16). We may not have access to the Sahara or the Sinai, or even to the Mojave or the Chihuahuan deserts, but we should be able to steal off to an uncluttered room, a quiet chapel or a prayerful place in nature in order to pray.

We learn the value of solitude by living. Specifically how God teaches us to enter into solitude is unique to each person. For some God uses the exuberating experience of success. For others he uses the wrenching experience of the cross to awaken them to the solitary dimension of life. For most of us God makes use of both successes and crosses to bring us to the more qualitative aspects of growth in him.

For example, we may spend a great deal of time, energy and resources pursuing our goal of becoming an accomplished musician, an excellent teacher, a skilled artist or a successful business person. Eventually we reach the top. What do we discover there? We find the need for something more. Even though we may experience fulfillment and satisfaction in our work sooner or later an inescapable emptiness asserts itself. We are driven to search further and deeper by a gnawing sense that surely there must be something more beyond this success.

[2]*Canticle*, 1, 6.
[3]See *Contemplation*, pp. 97-109, 126-131.

Moreover, we may be passionately in love with and loved by another person. Yet, no matter how beautiful and meaningful that relationship is, we will unavoidably begin to experience that emptiness which makes us search relentlessly for something more.

Through such positive experiences, the Spirit points us beyond ourselves to God. We taste firsthand our inability to be fully satisfied by anyone or anything other than God in himself. Some persons misinterpret at least for a while the specifically spiritual direction of this insatiable quest for something more. They fail to realize at first that this something is in fact some-One. So, it happens frequently that the one who has reached the top starts looking for more tops. The one who is restless in love may seek out another love (and another, and another). This can continue for a long time — even a lifetime — until finally we realize that: "You have made us for yourself, O Lord, and our heart is restless until it rests in you."[4] This experience constitutes the quintessence of solitude of heart.

With respect to the cross, we may, for instance, be struck down with a prolonged illness. We may find ourselves suddenly flat on our back, powerless to do anything. How are we to handle this unsought leisure? How are we to cope with this suffering?

The blows, the setbacks, the crises which occur in life teach us our helplessness, our dependency. In so doing, the cross drives us beyond ourselves and all our activities to God. It opens us to receive more fully his empowering love.[5]

Once we have had a sufficiently intense dose of solitude, from then on we know by personal experience the necessity and the value of solitude. After we have been sought out initially by solitude, we are then drawn spontaneously to seek it out. Gradually, the need for solitude parallels that of eating and sleeping. We may be able to skimp here and there.

---

[4]St. Augustine, *Confessions,* 1, 1 (*CCSL,* 27, 1. *PL* 32:661). See *Contemplation,* pp. 21-26; *Receptivity,* pp. 17-30, 85-88.

[5]See *Receptivity,* pp. 32-58, 63-82, 89-103, 106-109.

We can cut corners a while. But sooner or later it will catch up with us.

The deepening encounter with God in solitude wrenches forth in us an acute awareness of the abyss that exists between God and ourselves. In the light of Christ (*Jn* 8:12), we paradoxically experience light itself as darkness. As the light illumines the truth of our sinfulness, emptiness, dread, we cry out: "Oh, what a wretch I am!" (*Is* 6:5). "Who will save me from this body doomed to death?" (*Rm* 7:24).

Yet, in undergoing the anguish-filled, inner struggle between Christ and sin living within us, we experience also the life of the Spirit emerging through our death to self. In our poverty we realize profoundly the superabundant love and mercy of God. We are indeed sinners, but at the same time we are loved unconditionally and eternally by a tender Father (*Rm* 5:8).

Merton describes the inward journey of the true solitary in these terms: He "is a man of prayer.... He experiences in himself the emptiness, the lack of authenticity, the quest for fidelity, the 'lostness' of modern man." He "confronts his own humanity and that of his world at the deepest and most central point where the void seems to open out into black despair." He "confronts this serious possibility, and rejects it,... and transcends it by his freedom. The option of absolute despair is turned into perfect hope." He "faces the worst, and discovers in it the hope of the best. From the darkness comes light. From death, life. From the abyss there comes, unaccountably, the mysterious gift of the Spirit sent by God to make all things new, to transform the created and redeemed world, and to re-establish all things in Christ."[6]

Why then is solitude so essential for the spiritual director?

The response should be obvious. We cannot communicate a personal and loving God to another without having first experienced God as personal and loving. We cannot

[6]*C. Prayer*, p. 25.

give to another what we ourselves have not yet received. Mere knowledge *about* God does not suffice. We must know him personally, directly, by love and in faith. Thus, the first responsibility of an effective director is to attend to her/his own interior life, to take time for solitary prayer and for serious study.

In the experience of the desert, we receive from God the self-knowledge and the divine wisdom necessary for guiding directees. We must first be tempted in the desert (*Mt* 4:1). We need to have firsthand experience of our own human frailty being transformed by grace. We will never be able to direct another spiritually until we discover first our own spiritual direction. God does not play games. He does not cut corners. God fully expects that we let him make us worthy of the vocation to which we are called (*Eph* 4:1).

A director must therefore learn to be alone, to listen in inner stillness to the Spirit, to discover the truth about him/herself and God. The director's word to others will then be God's word. It will be a word of power — a word of inner authority (*Mt* 7:29) — because it will be a word out of silence and solitude and prayer.


## B. *Spiritual Persons:* Pneumatikoi

The desert fathers and mothers were spiritual persons in the full sense of the term. Abandoning themselves to God in faith, hope and love, they allowed their lives to be directed in every respect by the Spirit. The spiritualizing influence of God permeated the most sublime and the most mundane aspects of their lives. It attained every dimension of their personhood: emotional, psychological, physical, spiritual. The whole life of the abba or amma was in the process of spiritualization. Working, praying, recreating, they recognized all as having been received from God (1 *Co* 4:7). And they directed all that they had received back to the Father in loving abandonment.

The abbas and ammas lived freely, simply and spontaneously from the depths of their hearts. Therefore, the direction that they gave others was truly *spiritual* direction: that which they themselves first received from the Spirit and which in turn they imparted to others.

Like the desert fathers and mothers, directors are called by God to be spiritual persons in their own right, as well as spiritual directors.

There is a vast difference between a "natural" director and a truly "spiritual" director. Both profess to follow Christ, but one does so at some distance. The natural, sensate person — the *psychikos anthropos* — (1 *Co* 2:14) may be a truly good person, a great guy, a really fine woman. Yet, that still does not equal spiritual in the Pauline, desert or mystical sense. Such a person may well be full of spirit, but not necessarily of *the* Spirit. Such a director does not yet "accept those things which pertain to the Spirit of God, for they appear foolish to him/her. S/he cannot even know them, since they must be discerned spiritually. The spiritual person (*ho pneumatikos*), on the other hand, discerns all things" (1 *Co* 2:14-15), especially "the deep things of God" (1 *Co* 2:10-12).

The *psychikoi* discern reality according to external standards. They mistakenly measure their own spiritual progress, as well as that of others, by the degree of strict conformity to rules, regulations, customs and expectations of those in authority. The natural director "cannot liberate minds and heart, he cannot open them to the secret action of the Spirit. He trusts entirely in an external and legalistic knowledge of mere rudiments, and does not 'give life' or open up the way to genuine development."[7]

The *psychikoi*, fixated on the performance of external practices (like certain methods of prayer, set manners of communal living, rigid moral guidelines), block the life of the Spirit from flowing through them. They render themselves incapable of receiving anything of the Spirit. Anything of real spiritual value disturbs such persons. They cannot get a handle on it, and therefore conclude that it

[7]*S. Father*, p. 304.

must be "foolish" (1 *Co* 2:14). It does not fit into their preconceptions of who the Spirit should be and of how the Spirit should operate. Everything spiritual remains an enigma to the natural man or woman.

Cut off from the dynamic life of the indwelling Spirit, the *psychikoi* cannot discern reality by truly spiritual standards (1 *Co* 2:14). Those things which are in themselves of God, from God, to God have become their gods. They remain blinded by idols. Unfortunately, many who profess to be *good* Christians, *good* religious, *good* priests (or bishops) are little more than *psychikoi*.

The natural person who attempts spiritual direction will produce devastating effects. Having little or no experience of true spirituality, s/he will be unable to direct others spiritually and will be unable to understand the experience of persons who are deeply spiritual.

"By an insistence on non-essentials and by consistent neglect of the living needs of the disciples," the *psychikos* "tends to stifle life and to 'extinguish the Spirit.'" Although such a director may appear to love others, this love is but a disguised form of "his love for his own doctrine, his own ascetic system, 'his rule, his way'. He is capable of loving only those who acquiesce in his teaching.... He loves his disciples for the sake of his own doctrine, that is to say he makes use of the disciple to affirm the truth and rightness of his own system, or in the end, to show that he himself is a good director!"[8]

The *pneumatikoi* on the other hand, abandon themselves in faith, hope and love to the inscrutable ways of the Spirit. They seek only to let God be God and to let the Spirit blow wherever he wills, however he wishes. Spiritual persons are always at the disposal of God in mystery, always lovingly open and receptive, waiting on him with expectancy.

In guiding others, the spiritual director will thus be capable of loving directees with God's own love. S/he will have immense capacity to accept persons as they are, and will

[8] *S. Father*, p. 304.

spontaneously respect the unique way that the Spirit is spiritualizing each individual. Consequently, both the director's presence and words to a directee will spring from the root of tested love.

While living in the Spirit and allowing themselves to be directed towards ever greater spiritualization, spiritual directors are at the same time intensely involved in life and in all the endeavors of the world. They experience deeply the joys, the sorrows, the triumphs and the defeats which are integral to being and to becoming fully human. Teilhard de Chardin aptly reflects this truth: "As far as my strength will allow me —because I am a priest — I desire henceforth to be the first to become conscious of what the world loves, pursues, suffers; the first to seek, to sympathize, to toil; the first in self-fulfillment, the first in self-denial." I want to be "more widely human and more nobly terrestial than any servant of the world."⁹

Yet, in this immersion in creation, these spiritual persons pass all the way through themselves as well as through the events, persons and situations of life in order to discern God's presence at the core. The indwelling Spirit enables truly spiritual directors, to the extent that they possess purity of heart, to pierce through the maze of subtleties, ambiguities, illusions, contradictory feelings, etc., which so crowd in upon us, in order to see God transparent in life.

Furthermore, not only do spiritual persons perceive the presence of God in what appears good, but they also perceive the potential for good in all that is not yet good. Thus, a fundamental principle for spiritual directors is this: "God turns everything to the good of those who love him.... Nothing can separate us from the love of God made visible in Christ Jesus Our Lord" (*Rm* 8:28,39).

The perception of "God becoming all in all" (1 *Co* 15:28) enables spiritual directors to view the human condition in a transformed way. The experience of self, others and the world does not call forth a cynical, despairing attitude, but

⁹*The Priest* in *Writings in Time of War* (Harper, 1968), p. 222.

rather one of confidence and trust in the transforming love of God. The awareness of the creative power of God operative throughout the entirety of creation excites fresh hope, renewed meaning and vibrant possibility. Truly spiritual directors are empowered by the Spirit to communicate this transformed view of reality to others who sincerely seek their guidance.

## C. Sought Out by Others for Spiritual Guidance

In the early Church, many were lured by God into the desert, but not all were called to be abbas and ammas. A person may be quite holy, and yet not be called to the ministry of spiritual direction.

Those called to become abbas and ammas did not enter the desert *in order to* prepare themselves for this ministry. They sought the desert out of a burning desire to commune lovingly with God in silence and solitude. Yet, it was God's design that they should minister to others contemplatively inclined. Recognized for their personal experience of the Trinity as well as for their spiritual qualities, the desert fathers and mothers were sought out by other seekers of God.

The fact that they were indeed freely sought out pertains to the very core of what it means to be abba or amma. They did not presumptuously decide to direct others. They did not proudly set out on their own initiative to be spiritual masters or leaders. We never find a true abba or amma wandering around looking for someone to direct. Such behavior, if it occurs, would indicate either that one's so-called solitude is probably no more than an attempt to seek honor and glory by living differently from others, or at least that one is trying to escape the exigencies of the desert.

The abbas and ammas in fact did all within their power to live in obscurity and hiddenness. The more they were sought out, the more they risked going even further into the desert in order to secure the solitude they so desired.

Not that they begrudgingly gave of themselves to those who sought their assistance. On the contrary, they welcomed readily those who genuinely sought help, and ministered to them with deep love, compassion, gentleness and empathy. Nonetheless, this involvement with others had the positive effect of leading the desert solitaries to seek God even more ardently in solitude.

Actually, the fact that they were sought out by others was but the external sign that they possessed the God-given charism of engendering the life of the Spirit in those sent to them: The abba or amma "was one who was recognized as a charismatic and 'life-giving' influence, under whose care these mysterious seeds" of spiritual life "would truly grow and flourish."[10]

A person seeking spiritual direction from an abba or amma would ask for "a word." A word of insight, a word of encouragement. A word of counsel, a word of correction. The word of the spiritual father or mother would be expressive of God's will in the directee's concrete and unique situation.

The sayings which are preserved for us in the *Apothegmata* may have been the culmination of hours, weeks or even years of listening and discernment. They are principles for behavior and for attitudinal development. These logia synthesized and epitomized what the directee needed to hear.

Generally, the abbas and ammas present themselves as persons of very few words. Sometimes their very silence is their word. Consider for instance these two stories: (1) Some people had gathered at Scete. "They besought Abba Pambo: 'Speak a word to the Pope that he may be edified.' The old man replied: 'If he is not edified by my silence, he will not be edified by my speech either.'" (2) "Three persons visited Abba Anthony each year. Two of them used to question him about their thoughts and the salvation of their souls. The third, however, remained completely silent. After

[10] *S. Father*, p. 284.

a long while, Abba Anthony said to him, 'You have been coming to me all this time, yet you never ask me anything.' The other replied, 'Father, it is enough for me just to see you.'"[11]

The logia that do emerge out of this silent listening are simple, compact, to-the-point and charged with power to transform the sincere pilgrim. Take, for example, this logion addressed to a hermit who was probably tempted to seek diversion from the aridity of his hermitage: "A certain brother came to vist Abba Moses in Scete. He asked for a word. The old man said to him, 'Be gone. Sit in your cell and your cell will teach you everything you need to know.'" Amma Syncletica had this to say to one of her directees: "Imitate the publican, and you will not be condemned with the Pharisee [*Lk* 18:10-14]. Choose the meekness of Moses, and you will find the rock of your heart transformed into a spring of living water [*Nm* 20:11]."[12]

The life-engendering word of the abba or amma became a kind of personal rule whereby the disciple could live. The word expressed the particular way the pilgrim was to go forward in his/her journey to the Father.

The word given by the abba or amma was never exteriorly imposed or arbitrarily chosen. The logion emerged from the inner silence of the abba or amma wherein "it is not you who will be speaking. The Spirit of your Father will be speaking in you" (*Mt* 10:20). God used this word to bring into consciousness for the listener the direction which the Spirit was already indicating from within. "The impact of these 'words' resided not so much in their simple content as in the inward action of the Holy Spirit which accompanied them, in the soul of the hearer."[13]

What type of person sought out the desert fathers and mothers? It was the same sort of person who seeks spiritual direction today.

---

[11] *PG*, 65:198 (2) and 83 (27) respectively. See *Sayings*, pp. 69 and 6.

[12] *PG*, 65:283 (6) and 426 (11) respectively. See *Sayings*, pp. 118 and 195.

[13] *S. Direction*, p. 5.

They were above all those willing to face and to undergo the stark reality of their personal solitude. They were willing to submit themselves to the struggle unto death between God in them and sin in them in order that they would rise anew in Christ.

Without free, constant submission to God in the desert of their hearts any attempt to seek spiritual guidance would have been futile: "One might say that all other advice assumes that one is ready and willing to sustain the purifying silence and loneliness of the cell, in which one is stripped of his illusory image of himself and forced to come to terms with the nothingness, the limitation, the infidelity, the defectibility, or as we might say today the 'void' of his own life."[14]

Those who sought a word of salvation were deeply hungering and thirsting for God. They endeavored to discover their personal identities in Christ as well as to find the particular way they were each to attain him. They longed to go beyond the complacent, mediocre way of living which fettered them.

The disciples of the abbas and ammas were those who in experiencing themselves as poor, struggling and weak felt keenly their *need* for spiritual direction. They were the *anawim*: Blessed are those who know their need, for God is theirs and they are God's (*Mt* 5:3).

Merton sums up the interrelatedness of these elements (that is, the acceptance of personal solitude, a spirit of searching and a realization of one's need) in this manner: Spiritual direction "presupposes an ardent faith and a deep hunger for the word of God and for salvation. This spiritual appetite, this need for light, had in its turn been generated by tribulation and compunction. 'Direction' then was God's answer to a need created in the soul by trial and compunction, and communicated through a charismatic representative of the Mystical Body," an abba or amma.[15]

[14] S. *Father*, p. 295.
[15] S. *Direction*, p. 5.

A spiritual person is considered an abba or amma inasmuch as God prompts a directee to seek him/her out for spiritual direction. One is a spiritual father or mother to the degree that one is freely chosen, under the inspiration of the Spirit, by another as his/her spiritual guide. One is abba or amma to the extent that the directee is willing to become a child: that is, willing to submit to God through another in openness, trust and simplicity.

Thus, a basic sign of a call to become a spiritual director resides in the fact that one is sought out by others for spiritual direction. Initially, this encounter may occur spontaneously, without any formal agreement (or even explicit awareness) that a spiritual director-directee relationship is being engendered.

Being a spiritual director is a ministry, a charism in the strict sense. It is God-given primarily for the benefit of others. Becoming a spiritual director is something that happens. We do not set out to become a director. It occurs. It comes about in God's providence. With time and through sending persons to us, God awakens us to a consciousness of this call. He reveals our charism to us through individuals actually seeking out and finding spiritual direction from us.

The explicit awareness of the call to be spiritual director usually arises then from the experience of directing others, however limited or informal this experience may be. Perception of the call is thus generally the conscious realization of what is already to some extent taking place.

Nonetheless, the mere fact that we are sought out by others must not lead us to assume automatically that we are called by God to be spiritual directors. There are four areas of concern which would-be directors should explore in order to authenticate the presence of this charism:

*First*, we need to discern why we are being sought out. What are prospective directees seeking from us? Do they truly need and want spiritual direction, or are they looking for counseling, theological discussion, friendly conversation?

Is it that these people merely want to let off steam? Are we being asked to participate in a kind of faith sharing that attains neither the nature of spiritual direction nor the in-depth revelation of the other's person that spiritual direction requires? Are we being sought out for the intimate sharing and support that one gives a close friend? Spiritual direction may at times embrace some of the above. Nonetheless, there is an essential element to spiritual direction which transcends them all.

Furthermore, are we being sought out because of some unresolved weakness or personality disorder in us which attracts certain people? One  isolationist may seek out another isolationist as "director" because s/he intuits that his/her withdrawal will be left secure and unchallenged by such a person. A dependent personality may seek "direction" from a protective or mothering type.

Even a directee desirous of serious spiritual direction may be drawn to a certain director for questionable reasons: for example, because s/he is good-looking; because s/he strikes one's fancy; because the prospective director is a man and not a woman (or vice versa), a well-known author rather than a simple, ordinary person. These factors are part of the human condition. Yet, we have to address them and deal with them honestly. Otherwise the blind may end up leading the blind (*Mt* 15:14), and both may fall into the pit.

A *second* area worthy of note is this: Who is seeking us out for spiritual direction? Is it a particular type of person? For instance: only youth, married couples, celibates, priests, nuns, laity, contemplatives or beginners? Or, are we sought out by a wide range of people? Do people from a variety of backgrounds and lifestyles come to us? These questions should be explored in discerning to whom God may be sending us as spiritual directors. A spiritual director gives whatever assistance s/he can to each directee, but s/he may nonetheless be more competent with certain types of directees than with others.

A *third* consideration is the following: Is there indication that we are being called to spiritual direction as a full time ministry? Or, are we being called to integrate this ministry with other God-given responsibilities (for example: parent, pastor, nurse, professor, writer, administrator)?

*Finally*, we need to examine the fruits of the spiritual guidance which we impart. Over a reasonable period of time is there indication of authentic spiritual genesis in those whom we direct? If we are really called to give spiritual guidance, the Spirit will engender new life in those whom God sends us. A general lack of spiritual growth or evidence of deformation in our directees may indicate that the Spirit is not directing through us, and thus that we are not called to this ministry.

While the ministry of spiritual direction is principally for the good of others, God does not fail to use the charism itself for the director's own transformation and purification. This gift is necessarily integral to the director's personal life in faith. While always remaining a free gift, this charism is the normal outcome of one's own spiritual genesis, and it is an important instrument for further personal spiritualization.

At least initially, it is prudent for a new director to seek guidance from a more experienced director. Personal study of the scriptures, theology and related disciplines also enhances greatly a director's competency. Furthermore, undergoing the experience of being directed by another can prove invaluable for any director. This is beneficial both from the point of view of personal spiritual growth as well as that of learning firsthand what constitutes authentic spiritual direction.

*Chapter 4*

# Spiritual Direction as Listening

The formation of a spiritual director-directee relationship is the result of a twofold call: God calls a particular directee to a certain director, and vice versa. The spiritual director and the directee are sent to each other so that united in the same Spirit they may together listen to God within the directee.

The mystery of this twofold call becomes actualized through the convergence of two factors: (1) the consciousness within a person of a need for spiritual guidance, plus (2) the availability of a spiritual director to whom one is drawn. Without the concurrence of both these conditions, the relationship cannot be established.

## A. The Directee's Need for a Spiritual Director

God sows the seed of this relationship by awakening prospective directees through the ordinary circumstances of their lives to the fact that they need the assistance of another person in discerning their spiritual direction. Grace directs them to avail themselves of the mediation of another, and to listen to and obey God speaking through him/her.

At the outset, the realization of this need is sometimes triggered by a specific problem or personal crisis. Frequently, however, directees have no more than a vague realization that they need help, without being able to identify any particular difficulty. It is this experience of a personal need for spiritual guidance which incites them to look for a spiritual director.

Although directees feel or think that they need a director, this fact does not necessarily mean that God is indeed calling them to receive guidance in this manner. Their feelings and thoughts could arise from a craving to know answers, from a desire for certitude and control, from an impatience with abiding in mystery. Curiosity or the quest for consolation leads some persons to seek a director. Still others want a director as a status symbol.

Unless God desires that directees have a spiritual director, he will not provide one. No matter how much they seek or even demand a director, none will be forthcoming. In fact, if the initiation of meetings with some director proceeds solely from them, these directees will find themselves incapable of receiving spiritual direction. Their efforts to create a director-directee relationship on their own will be frustrated at every turn.

Sometimes though, directees experience an authentic need for spiritual direction, and discover that despite all their searching no suitable director is available. In this instance, God himself will surely provide the necessary direction through some other means: for example, the sacraments, homilies, spiritual reading, a chance encounter, interior inspiration.

Nonetheless, if directees experience a real need for a spiritual director, they must not claim too readily that they are unable to find one. "Some who lament the fact that they cannot find a director actually have all the opportunities for direction they really need, but they are not pleased with the available director because he does not flatter their self-esteem or cater to their illusions about themselves. In other words, they want a director who will confirm their hope of finding pleasure in themselves and in their virtues, rather than one who will strip them of self-love and show them how to get free from preoccupation with themselves and their own petty concerns."[1]

In discerning which director to choose, it is important to consider the necessary qualifications for this ministry: personal experience of God, competency in ascetical-mystical theology, ability to discern, etc. Ultimately, however, it is by faith that directees recognize intuitively the appropriate director. They find themselves drawn subtly, mysteriously to one person. There may be several other directors available. Some may be more learned, more gifted or apparently more prayerful. Yet, directees recognize intuitively and in faith the one to whom God is sending them.

Intuition must, of course, be tested. Are they drawn to a certain director primarily because s/he is popular or held in high esteem? Are they merely following the crowd, jumping on the latest bandwagon? Do they want this person to be their director because they expect him/her to be easy? Are they seeking some form of self-gratification? Is their claim to be seeking direction a guise to pursue a strong natural attraction for some individual? Are they trying to establish a director-directee relationship as a misdirected way of seeking intimate friendship? Needless to say, God can use even misguided motives to bring a person to the proper director.

In some instances, directees may find a spiritual director almost as soon as they begin looking. Often, however, the appropriate director is not immediately available. In fact, it may be quite some time — perhaps even years — before the director to whom God is sending them enters their lives. When there is such a delay, they should remain open and wait patiently, always alert and watchful for the right person (*Mt* 24:44).

---

[1] *S. Direction*, p. 22.

## B. The Director's Discernment of the Directee's Need

When a directee first approaches us to be his/her spiritual director, discernment is necessary also on our part. Are there indications of a God-given call to guide this person? The presence of mutual trust and confidence is surely a positive sign. Furthermore, in the light of existing commitments and responsibilities do we have the time and energy to take on another directee? In the last analysis, however, we too will have to rely on intuition enlightened by faith to discern the authenticity of this mysterious call.

At the outset, directors should reflect as well on the following questions:

(1) Are prospective directees seeking spiritual direction in the strict sense? What is their understanding of spiritual direction? Sometimes, people think they want spiritual direction. Yet, when we probe further, we discover that they are in fact looking for something quite other: counseling, affirmation, someone to talk to. Other times, what they really want is little more than a kind of friendly sharing in which the director gives approval and agreement, without question or challenge.

The true intentions of such persons are usually not long in becoming manifest. In the actual imparting of spiritual direction — for instance, a specific suggestion for solitary prayer — we begin sensing resistance and rebellion in them. They may act as if they have been affronted, or claim their privacy has been invaded. They may accuse us of talking down to them, and insist that we do not have sufficient knowledge of their lives to offer specific guidance. Obviously, there is no way a spiritual director-directee relationship can be maintained as long as these attitudes persist.

(2) Have directees exercised freedom in choosing their director? For the spiritual director-directee relationship to be effective, freedom is essential.

Occasionally, persons seek direction primarily because they are pressured to do so, either subtly or overtly, by a well-meaning superior, friend or spouse. Sent to a particular director against their wishes, they find it very difficult, if not impossible, to be open and frank. Sometimes others need to encourage and even persuade a person to pursue spiritual direction. But no one should ever be forced.

Once in a while we discover that we are in fact a directee's second choice. Because the preferred director appears busy, overburdened or uninviting, the directee may not approach him/her for guidance. Sometimes too, a directee is so confused over questions of proper motivation that s/he is not aware that a certain director is indeed his/her second choice. Ordinarily in these instances we should help such directees discern the authenticity of their primary choice, and encourage them to act upon it when appropriate.

What about being assigned a director? This case arises especially in institutions of formation, renewal and retreat. Naturally, prudence must be exercised.

In assigning a director the following principles are to be considered: (1) Spiritual direction cannot be forced on persons who do not want it. In some instances, it may be necessary to inform certain individuals that without spiritual direction they may not remain at the given retreat house or house of prayer. However, whether or not they avail themselves of direction has to be their own choice. (2) Before making the assignment, the person responsible for this task should receive some basic knowledge of each directee's needs so that the proper director can be matched with those needs. (3) Directees have to be willing to go to their assigned director even though they may not be acquainted with him/her. (4) Should a directee discover that s/he cannot open up to an assigned director despite the good will and sincerity of both, the possibility of discontinuing spiritual direction or of changing to another director should exist.

God can certainly use any of the preceding instances as a providential way of bringing directees to *his* choice of director for them. Yet, for a true spiritual director-directee relationship to evolve, at some point in the encounter the directee must freely choose the spiritual director and the director freely accept the call.

## C. The Director-Directee Relationship: Grounded in God-Centered Listening

From the outset, the director-directee relationship has to be centered on God in such a way that each is listening to God in the other. The relationship must be God-centered because it is only in him that each encounters what God has in store for the other.

### (1) PSYCHOLOGICAL DIMENSIONS OF LISTENING

On a psychological level, the quality of personal interaction in the director-directee relationship is dependent on at least three factors: (a) the ability of each to arrive at self-intimacy, (b) the recognition that each person is different, (c) the capacity to listen to each other.

### (a) The Ability of Each to Arrive at Self-Intimacy

Self-intimacy is the ability to listen to ourselves in all the diverse facets of our being. It is to experience the mystery of ourselves as we really are. Self-intimacy means being attuned to whatever promotes in a responsible way our physical, mental, emotional, spiritual health and well-being. It predicates ownership of our thoughts, feelings, desires, aspirations and motives.

Self-intimacy facilitates the discovery and the development of our creative potential: our talents, gifts, strengths. Yet, self-intimacy confronts us also with the unavoidable truth of our sinfulness and weakness despite our best efforts and intentions.

Self-intimacy in no way implies narcissistic fixation on self. Rather it is a communion with self that thrusts us into communion with others and especially with God. Self-intimacy is the effect of mature love of self. As such, it is the direct opposite of self-centeredness. Indeed, self-intimacy is quite selfless in the moral sense. Our capacity to love others is profoundly related to our ability to love ourselves: "Love your neighbor as yourself" (*Mt* 22:39; *Lv* 19:18).

The recognition and the responsible satisfaction of our personal needs — whether physical, mental, emotional or spiritual — awaken an awareness of the needs of those around us. Self-intimacy enables us to see others as another self. Thus, we quicken our receptivity to others and we are more able to give of ourselves in order to promote what is to their benefit.

Self-intimacy increases our capacity to be productive members of society, to make prudent judgments, decisions and moral choices. It enables us to attain insight, to interpret events more correctly and to act in a manner that is responsible and accountable.

The self-acceptance that grows through self-intimacy leads to acceptance of others. Self-acceptance makes us more aware of their strengths as well as more patient and tolerant with their weaknesses.

Above all, intimacy with self enables us to face the inescapable solitary dimension of our lives. Self-intimacy inevitably confronts us with our aloneness. Before we can stand being alone before God, we have to be at home being alone with ourselves. Not only must we be at ease with leisure and solitude, but also we have to experience our inner need and longing for it. Our ability to welcome and foster solitude in our life is paradoxically the basis of all personalism and altruism. In short, the discovery of solitude opens us to deeper intimacy with self, others and God.

Quite the contrary is the person who is alienated from self. Self-alienation occurs when we deny or repress our inner experience of selfhood and of our world. Because of fear or lack of self-acceptance, we block off our true feelings and inspirations while attempting to substitute something false in their place. Trying to be someone we are not, we interact with our world by constantly changing masks. Refusing to be who we are, we persist in playing some imaginary role that appears appropriate. We become haunted by anxiety and guilt arising from the fact that we are living a pretense, a lie. To others our behavior may appear adolescent, immature, inconsistent, irresponsible. Within us abides the fear that we may not be successful in maintaining our act. We develop feelings of insecurity, inadequacy and inferiority. Frequently, these attitudes result in such self-destructive behavior as overwork, compulsive eating or smoking, drug or alcohol addiction, accident proneness, even suicide.

Self-alienation has particularly devastating effects on our ability to be intimate with others: "Alienation from self increases the need to be loved and accepted but decreases the capacity to love. Self-hatred erects a barrier to satisfactory relationships. When an individual hates himself or herself, he or she operates by means of pretense and deceit. Since these means cannot be hidden from self, contempt for self increases. Self-contempt, self-alienation, and self-hatred are expressed in hostility towards others. Such hostility breeds so much anxiety and guilt that an individual finds it impossible to enjoy any relationship at all," even with God.[2]

At the core of self-love, self-intimacy, self-acceptance is the ability to listen attentively — listen to self, to others, to God in any situation.

### (b) The Recognition of Basic Differences and Uniqueness

Every person possesses a unique personality and is called to personal fulfillment in a singular way. Each person has different strengths and weaknesses as well as a completely different life history. Even if they have spent their entire lives in the same family, social or ecclesial context, any two individuals have unique personal experiences of life. Any interpersonal encounter, if it is to be authentic, must be based on the recognition that we are each essentially different and distinct persons.

A meaningful relationship begins with the recognition that we cannot exactly understand one another. Even in a deep, long-standing, loving relationship, one person can

---

[2]Philomena Agudo, "Intimacy with Self vs. Self-Alienation" in *Intimacy* (Affirmation Books, 1978) pp. 20-21. See *idem*, pp. 15-23; Eric Fromm, *The Art of Loving* (Harper, 1956).

never completely exhaust the unknown, mysterious element of the other. In fact, the more two people are united in love, the more distinctly they each develop in becoming one. Love differentiates. At the same time that it unites, love awakens in each person the maximum of his/her individuality and uniqueness. Thus, we enter into any relationship with this truth in mind: I do not and cannot understand you exactly. Indeed, I cannot even understand myself entirely (*Rm* 7:15).

In a growing relationship with another, we discover quickly mutual affinities and similarities. Yet, if we do not also recognize the complementary and unitive aspects of fundamental differences, we drift towards mutual absorption and loss of personal identity. Seeing the other too much as an extension of self leads us to expect the other to feel, think, respond exactly as we ourselves do. These unrealistic expectations engender anxiety and frustration since the other person — simply because s/he is necessarily different — cannot possibly fulfill them.

When we encounter another person, a confrontation of two inner worlds occurs. We are faced with a dynamic, personal and particular world that stands out against our own. It does so not in direct opposition to our world, but simply by the fact that we are not the other person and his/her world is not ours.

Since we are so fundamentally different, how can we possibly commune? How are we to penetrate each other's world of experience? Only by listening to each other!

### (c) The Capacity to Listen to Another

Listening is the basis of all personal interaction.[3]

No communication can occur until at least one person becomes a listener. If both are always speakers, each persists in talking from his/her own world of experience without any attempt to enter into the experience of the other. Should

---

[3]See Eugene Kennedy, *On Becoming a Counselor* (Seabury, 1977) pp. 3-59; Marc Oraison, *Being Together* (Doubleday, 1970); Earl Koile, *Listening as a Way of Becoming* (Regency, 1977).

one person listen, s/ he can share in the life of the other. Yet, human interaction transpires most effectively when both persons are listeners. Speaking then arises from listening. It invites deeper listening. In this way, the possibility exists for that mutual communing in which two persons encounter each other in love at their most sublime and mysterious depths.

By listening, we leave our own world of experience in order to put ourselves into that of the other. We wear the other's hat, as it were. We walk in the other's shoes. Listening requires a giving of oneself in the very act of receiving the gift of the other. A veritable self-emptying is integral to listening to another person. The example par excellence of this truth is the kenosis of Jesus. Listening to our need for salvation necessitated his emptying himself of his own world of divine experience in order to become human (*Ph* 2:6-8).

To be at the disposal of another by listening, we have to let go our world of experience: our struggles, our joys, our concerns, our cares. We must even let go of any tendency to judge the other by our principles, our convictions, our moral code. This letting go happens in such a way that we never cease being who we really are. Thus, it is not a question of being the other, but rather of being oneself to the other.

Listening then is the attentiveness of our being to another's becoming in all his/ her beauty and sinfulness, struggle and mystery. It is a surrender of ourselves in love to another person. Listening is being with another in loving attentiveness to that which is most mysterious, elusive and ineffable in the other. Listening is necessarily believing in another.[4]

Thus, even in the psychological realm listening pertains to the personal. We do not listen to some-thing. Even though we may hear something, if we listen at all, we listen to some-one: to a person.

---

[4]See *Receptivity*, pp. 49-53, 97-101.

## (2) SPIRITUAL DIMENSIONS OF LISTENING

While the relationship between the director and the directee encompasses the psychological dimensions discussed above, there is an aspect to spiritual direction which transcends completely the psychological as such. This relationship presupposes that both the director and the directee are capable of self-intimacy, of the recognition of their essential differences and of listening to each other. Yet, spiritual direction goes beyond all this. It is a listening together by the director and the directee to God within the directee.

Frequently God implores his people to listen to him: "Listen, Oh Israel" (*Dt* 6:4). "Listen, listen to me.... Pay attention, come to me. Listen and your soul will live" (*Is* 55:2-3). "Listen to my voice. Then I shall be your God and you will be my people" (*Jr* 7:23). "This is my beloved Son.... Listen to him"(*Mk* 9:7). "Listen to me, all of you, and understand" (*Mk* 7:14). "Let anyone who listens answer, 'Come'"(*Rv* 22:17). "The Holy Spirit says: 'If today you listen to his voice, harden not your hearts'" (*Hb* 3:7). "Listen anyone who has ears!" (*Mt* 13:9).

Samuel acknowledges that he is truly in tune with God: "Speak, Lord, your servant is listening" (1 *Sm* 3:10). Solomon asks Yahweh for a most special gift: "Give your servant a listening heart (*lebh shomea*) so as to be able to discern" (1 *Kg* 3:9).

Jesus himself admonishes those unable to listen: "The one belonging to God listens to his words. If you refuse to listen, it is because you are not of God" (*Jn* 8:47). "Everyone who listens to these words of mine, but does not act on them is like a fool" (*Mt* 7:26). "I have told you already, and you did not listen. Why do you want to hear it again?" (*Jn* 9:27).

There are also examples of persons who do in fact listen to Jesus: "In the early morning people came to him in the Temple to listen to him"(*Lk* 21:38). "Mary sat down at the Lord's feet and listened to his word"(*Lk* 10:39). "All who are on the side of truth listen to my voice"(*Jn* 18:37). "The sheep that belong to me listen to my voice" (*Jn* 10:27).

In the scriptures two verbs are used consistently to express listening: the Hebrew *shama* and the Greek *akouo*. Very possibly, both *shama* and *akouo* originally denoted little more than receiving input from an external source through the sense of hearing. Gradually, however, these verbs took on a more spiritual and theological nuance. Rather than stressing the act of hearing what someone says, *shama* and *akouo* came to accentuate principally the idea of listening to someone: a person. We *hear* noises, sounds, voices. But we *listen* to a person. Take the example of music. We can hear music: at a distance, in the background, the sounds of its instruments. Or, we can listen to music. That is, we can let our souls get in touch with its soul. When we listen to music, we somehow commune with someone through it, beyond it.

Listening denotes interpersonal communion. Listening can be so personal in fact that words do not have to be uttered. Listening is akin to empathy wherein two persons commune in love, without necessarily hearing or doing a thing. Listening implies receiving the other into oneself.

Both *shama* and *akouo*, in their deepest sense, describe a quality that is integral to all loving, interpersonal communion between God and the human person. Listening to God is a fundamental stance required of a child in relation to his/her Father.

Listening is that attitude of heart whereby that which is deepest and most mysterious in us remains in loving attentiveness to that which is deepest and most mysterious in God. By listening, we abide in the simplicity of being in love with our God. We remain loving our Beloved with our whole heart, soul, mind and strength (*Mt* 22:37), irrespective of words, thoughts and specific actions.

Listening is unconditional surrender to *Abba*. Listening is a giving of our deepest to him whose depth has no end. Thus, it is an act of abandonment in faith, hope and love, a wordless, imageless, loving surrender of our whole being to God.

Listening is waiting upon God in watchful expectancy. Not that we wait for or expect some-*thing*. Rather we wait for some-*One*: God himself.

There is, therefore, a future as well as a realized eschatological element in listening to God. Above all, we remain loving and being loved by our Beloved. Yet, at the same time we are seeking after and being sought out by the One whom we do not completely possess. Consequently, listening holds within itself the tension integral to all love this side of the resurrection: that of simultaneously abiding in the One we love and undergoing the passionate longing, yearning and desire for the same One we await.

In the context of spiritual direction then, listening is the basic stance of the director and the directee towards God. It is not enough that a director and a directee listen to each other. Together they must listen to God himself giving the directee spiritual direction. Listening establishes communion with God wherein both remain attentive to him in dark faith, complete trust, unconditional love. Listening is a waiting together on God in vigilant expectancy, sheer receptivity and unrestricted openness, irrespective of particular words, thoughts, gestures or feelings.

Listening is an act of faith in which the director and the directee surrender their deepest selves in mystery to ineffable Love. By listening, they remain loving their Beloved in naked abandonment. They are so abandoned to him that they let go all desire to see, feel, hear, understand anything at all.

Listening to God, like loving, has within itself its own reason for being. The director and the directee do not listen *in order to* receive some particular message, feeling or communication. "In a certain sense, we must truly begin to hear God when we have ceased to listen" for any thing. "What is the explanation of this paradox? Perhaps only that there is a higher kind of listening, which is not an attentiveness to some special wave length, a receptivity to a certain kind of message, but a general emptiness that waits to realize the fullness of the message of God within its own apparent void.”[5]

No, listening is not directed towards attaining some-*thing*. We listen to some-One, without necessarily having a reason or a purpose beyond the person we are listening to. “The true contemplative is not one who prepares his mind for a particular message that he wants or expects to hear, but who remains empty because he knows that he can never expect or anticipate the word that will transform his darkness into light. He does not even anticipate a special kind of transformation. He does not demand light instead of darkness. He waits on the Word of God in silence.”[6]

The director listening together with the directee to the indwelling Word will at times also hear something: particular insights, inspirations, words. Various feelings, questions, anxieties may also emerge while listening to God. Sometimes the director and the directee feel that God is present to them. They feel peace and joy. On other occasions they feel God’s apparent absence. They experience confusion, turmoil, struggle in listening. Oftentimes too, they understand that God is asking something specific of the directee, or they receive some particular self-knowledge.

Whether or not anything tangible emerges in listening to God is entirely the Father’s business (*Lk* 2:49). It depends wholly on what God wills at a given moment. Nor is it better in spiritual direction to receive something observable or to receive nothing at all. What is best is that the director and the directee always listen to God the way he desires: hearing *todo* or hearing *nada*.

This may indeed be a difficult and paradoxical truth to implement. While often it is the awareness of a specific need that leads the directee to seek direction in the first place, authentic spiritual direction cannot transpire if resolving that need, looking for that answer, getting that quick solu-

[5]*C. Prayer*, p. 90. See *Contemplation*, pp. 146-147.
[6]*C. Prayer*, p. 90.

tion become the prime focus. To do so would be to center upon some-*thing* rather than to listen to God.

If we truly listen to God, free from all desire to feel, to know, to be in control, to see clearly the way, we will then be properly disposed to receive any spiritual direction the Spirit may give. Set your heart on God and everything else will be given to you as well (*Lk* 12:31).

Even when the directee receives some-*thing* in spiritual direction —through listening to God — this still pertains to the realm of the personal. The "way" which is indicated, the "truth" which is revealed, the "life" which is awakened is but a concrete, specific manner of converging more fully upon the person of Christ Jesus who is the Way, the Truth and the Life (*Jn* 14:6).

It must be further emphasized that the listening to God which is the essence of spiritual direction is a listening to God *within* the directee: "The Word, the Son of God, together with the Father and the Holy Spirit, is hidden in essence and in presence in the innermost being of the soul."[7] It is there above all that he must be sought.

Thus, the accent in spiritual direction is on interiority. God is the source and ground of our being. It is from within that he is recreating us in his own image and likeness. Consequently, the directee's spiritual direction must be sought within the directee him/herself.

How do we discover God within ourselves? It is principally through our self-experience that we discover the indwelling Father, Son and Spirit. We find God by passing all the way through ourselves to him who dwells in our inmost being: "We know him in so far as we become aware of ourselves as known through and through by him. We 'possess' him in proportion as we realize ourselves to be possessed by him in the inmost depths of our being....Our knowledge of God is paradoxically a knowledge not of him as the object of our scrutiny, but of ourselves as utterly dependent on his saving and merciful knowledge of us... We

---

[7]*Canticle*, 1, 6. See *Receptivity*, pp. 18-23.

know him in and through ourselves in so far as his truth is the source of our being and his merciful love is the very heart of our life and existence."[8]

Spiritual direction then is concerned with discerning the spiritualizing influence of God within the directee as manifested in and through his/her thoughts, feelings, desires, aspirations, activities and relationships. "Let me know myself, Oh Lord, that I may know you."[9] The director and the directee listening together to God discern his influence within the directee as well as the spiritualizing direction he indicates.

For the directee, therefore, spiritual direction emerges from listening to God within him/herself and also from listening to God in and through the director. A spiritual director gives direction as a consequence of having listened to God within and through the directee. "It is God only that internally teaches both the teacher and disciple and his inspirations are the only lesson for both."[10]

[8]*C. Prayer*, p. 83.
[9]St. Augustine, *Soliloquies*, 2, 1, (*PL*, 32:885).
[10]*H. Wisdom*, p. 41.

## Chapter 5

# Manifestation of the Heart

One frequently hears questions like these: What should I tell my director? What am I supposed to say? Such questions imply mistaken attitudes towards spiritual direction itself. They can suggest a preoccupation with what some directees assume must be a fixed method for conducting spiritual direction, or they can indicate a desire to placate the director by acquiescing to what directees imagine are his/her expectations.

In deep spiritual direction there is nothing that the directee should or is supposed to say. There are no self-imposed or a priori expectations in that sense. All that is required is that directees reveal to their directors as simply, as honestly and as frankly as possible the stirrings of their heart. Some classical authors refer to this disclosure as "manifestation of thoughts" or "manifestation of conscience." We prefer the phrase "manifestation of the heart."

Throughout the history of spirituality, the great masters have consistently counseled in this vein: "Lay bare your wound to your spiritual physician. Without being ashamed say: 'Here is my fault, Father. Here is my illness.'"[1]

[1]St. John Climacus, *Ladder*, 4 (*PG*, 88:709-710).

Admonishing the young monk to reveal the secrets of his heart, St. Basil urges: "If he wants to make any progress he must not conceal any movement of his soul....Rather he should reveal the secrets of his heart to those of his brothers whose office it is to exercise a compassionate and sympathetic solicitude for the weak. In this way, what is laudable will be ratified, and what is reprehensible will receive the correction it deserves. By practicing such openness, we shall gradually be made perfect."[2]

St. Francis de Sales advises in similar fashion: "Open your heart" to your director "with all sincerity and fidelity, manifesting clearly and explicitly the state of your conscience without fiction or pretense. In this way your good actions will be examined and approved. Your evil ones will be corrected and remedied. You will be comforted and strengthened in your afflictions, moderated and regulated in your consolations."[3]

## A. The Heart

Why such insistence on revealing the heart? What is there about the heart that is so integral to spiritual direction?

In its biblical sense, heart denotes the whole person, with particular accent on one's inmost affective being. In the heart dwell feelings and emotions, desires and passions. The heart is the seat of wisdom and the source of understanding. It is the locus of the will and the spring from which moral conduct flows. It is within the heart that God himself must dwell.

God seeks out his chosen ones particularly in the heart: "You shall love Yahweh your God with all your heart" (*Dt* 6:5). "Deep within them I will plant my Law, writing it upon their hearts" (*Jr* 31:33). "I am going to lure her out into the desert and commune with her heart" (*Ho* 2:16).

---

[2] *The Long Rules,* 26 (*PG,* 31:985-988).
[3] *Introduction to the Devout Life,* 1, 4.

It is specifically the hearts of his people that God calls to conversion: "If you seek the Lord with all your heart and with all your soul, you will find him" (*Dt* 4:29). "Come back to me with all your heart....Let your hearts be opened, not your garments torn. Return to Yahweh your God" (*Jl* 2:12-13).

The heart is the place in which God recreates us in his own image and likeness, transforming and purging us: "Yahweh, your God, will circumcise your heart... until you love him with all your heart" (*Dt* 30:6). "I shall give you a new heart and put a new spirit in you. I shall remove your heart of stone and give you a heart of flesh instead" (*Ez* 36:26). "Create in me, Oh God, a cleansed heart. Renew a steadfast spirit within me" (*Ps* 51:10).

Yahweh examines the heart: "Remember how Yahweh your God led you for forty years in the desert to test you and to know your inmost heart" (*Dt* 8:2). "You probe my heart, Oh Lord, and examine me at night. You test me" (*Ps* 17:3).

Yahweh knows intimately every heart: "A man's conduct may strike him as upright. Yahweh, however, tries the heart" (*Pr* 21:2). "Sheol and the Abyss lie open to Yahweh. How much more the hearts of humankind!" (*Pr* 15:11).

Furthermore, God unites the hearts of his people to himself: "May your hearts be entirely with Yahweh your God" (1 *Kg* 8:61). God creates within a person the desire to love and to serve him single-heartedly: "Yahweh, teach me your way that I may walk beside you faithfully. Make my heart one that it may reverence your name" (*Ps* 86:11).

The heart then is above all the place of sacred encounter between the human person and God. It is actually in the heart that God dwells: "The love of God has been poured into our hearts by the Holy Spirit" (*Rm* 5:5). "God has sent the Spirit of his Son into our hearts" (*Ga* 4:6). "May the Lord direct your hearts in the love of God" (2 *Th* 3:5). Jesus himself proclaims: "Blessed are the pure in heart, for they shall see God" (*Mt* 5:8).

Yet, the human heart is also the source of much ache: "The heart is more devious than anything else and desperately sick. Who can understand it?" (*Jr* 17:9). It is from within the heart that inordinate desires and behavior flow: "What proceeds out of the mouth comes from the heart. This is what defiles a person" (*Mt* 15:18). "The good draw what is good out of the good treasure in their heart. The wicked draw evil from the evil in their hearts. Words flow out of what fills the heart" (*Lk* 6:45). "It is from within, from out of our hearts, that evil thoughts, fornication, theft, murder, adultery, avarice, malice, deceit, indecency, envy, slander, pride, folly emerge" (*Mk* 7:21-22).

Within each human heart there exists this paradox: Christ lives in us, in our spiritual selves; and sin lives in us, in our fleshy selves (*Ga* 2:20; *Rm* 7:14-17). Although Christ dwells within us transforming us into his likeness (2 *Co* 3:18), this side of the resurrection sin also dwells in us. The heart is enflamed with a divine restlessness which thrusts it forward in Christ. Yet, at the same time it is drawn inward upon itself, thus cutting itself off from Christ.

St. Paul captures vividly the inner struggle and tension which result from this situation: "Every single time I want to do good it is something evil that comes to hand. In my deepest self I delight in God's Law, but I can see that my body follows a law different from the one my reason dictates" (*Rm* 7:22-23).

We live in Christ. Yet, we lack complete transformation in him. Because both Christ and sin live in us, discernment between the two is paramount: "You must discover what the Lord wants of you" (*Eph* 5:10). "We know that God lives in us by the Spirit whom he has given us. Yet, it is not every spirit that you can trust. Test them to see if they come from God" (1 *Jn* 3:24-4:1). "Test yourselves to make sure that you are in the faith" (2 *Co* 13:5).

## B. Baring One's Heart

Ultimately, to manifest one's heart to one's director means to lay bare all that one truly desires. Directees have to be able to reveal the secret aspirations which they cherish in their hearts, since their hearts are the secret refuge to which they can escape. Directees must be able to lay bare their hearts, knowing full well that in manifesting them they risk encountering reality in a different light.

The truth stated above implies an important principle: namely, in the basic decisions of life, God moves persons to will freely whatever he wills for them. Because of the uniqueness of every person, each directee manifests something of God which is utterly singular in all creation. Each has something to say of God which has never been said before and which will never be repeated in exactly the same way. All that pertains to a directee's personality, vocation, mission converge upon and dialogue with this uniqueness. No person can become fully individualized until s/he is allowed to become his/her own person. In spiritual direction, then, it is of the utmost importance to discover what directees truly desire in order to discern what God actually wills for them.

This, however, is no easy task, since directees want all kinds of things which have little or nothing to do with their fundamental desire. There are situations in which they do not even want at all what their deepest being desires. They want to know, to possess, to control. Their pride drives them to manipulate, to force, to dominate. They crave to feel God in some sensory way, to cling to something created. If directees are to pass beyond all immature wishes, wants and "gim-me's" to their pristine desire, they must heed the advice of St. John of the Cross:

"In order to experience pleasure in all (*todo*),
Desire to have pleasure in nothing (*nada*).
In order to arrive at possessing all,
Desire to possess nothing.
In order to arrive at being all,
Desire to be nothing.
In order to arrive at knowing all
Desire to know nothing."[4]

[4]*Ascent*, I, 13, 11. See *Receptivity*, pp. 15-16, 44-48.

Only by honestly recognizing their spontaneous desires and by manifesting them to their directors can directees discern the origin of these yearnings and the direction which they indicate.

In spiritual direction, manifestation of the heart is obviously an important instrument in discernment. However, as essential as it remains, it can at times be quite difficult to accomplish.

## (1) OBSTACLES TO OPENNESS

When directees open their heart to the director, they stand exposed before him/her in naked truth. To stand before another just as God sees them is a formidable risk. It is to let go all facades and defenses. It is to leave themselves open and vulnerable to possible misunderstanding or rejection. Most people cringe before such a task.

Reluctance to manifest their heart to the director may stem from many causes: lack of self-esteem, pride, shyness, nervousness. Fear or avoidance of the truth and of its consequences is a common occurrence. Usually the very fact that persons seek out direction indicates a basic sincerity in pursuing truth. But the thorny question remains: Just how much truth do they really want to know? Are they unconditionally willing to receive whatever God wants to reveal? Or, have they consciously or unconsciously set limits to their openness?

Even sincere directees who are basically conscientious about manifestation of the heart attempt occasionally to avoid the whole truth and try to hide it from their director. These tendencies are evident in certain defense mechanisms which directees sometimes employ.

In order to steer discussion away from the real issues, directees may, for example, attempt to strike up a casual conversation with the director about work, family, community, recreational activities or mutual acquaintances. Another effective diversionary tactic is to draw him/her into a discussion about mutual convictions, principles or values. Directees get the director so involved in these issues that before they know it, the time has come to terminate their meeting.

Again, directees may seek to conceal themselves by focusing undue attention on the private life of the director. This may take the form of asking personal questions and making observations about his/her family or background. They may try to sidetrack the director by lavishing praise and flattery upon him/her. Or, they may deliberately provoke defensiveness in the director by criticizing or by otherwise drawing attention to his/her weaknesses and insufficiencies. At times also, directees dodge the truth by claiming that they are being misunderstood. They then insist on rehashing the nonthreatening aspects of their lives, sometimes ad nauseam.

To avoid revealing themselves, directees may arrive a little late for an appointment. If the desire for avoidance is strong enough, they may even conveniently forget to show up at all or cancel the appointment on some pretext.

Extreme secretiveness in regard to any aspect of personal life, as well as deliberately withholding from the director anything that has bearing on the interior life, obstructs the listening process. Some directees are especially tempted to withhold information when a sexual problem is involved: for example, homosexuality, autoeroticism, physical intimacies.

If the director makes an observation or gives advice that they do not like, directees may try to block it out. They may manage a smile and maintain all the social niceties, possibly agreeing verbally with the director. Yet, inside they erect barriers to prevent the director's words from penetrating their heart. They may have even developed an elaborate system of rationalization for this behavior. These directees say to themselves: The director is not as spiritual as I am. The director is closed-minded, judgmental. What the director speaks is merely his/her opinion. In these instances, the director often has the impression of being shut out, of being up against a stone wall.

Another common defense mechanism is that of intellectualization. Directees avoid manifestation of the heart by intellectualizing about prayer, love, life, personal relationships. For example, when asked to describe their solitary prayer, they take a scriptural text that they used for meditation. They then proceed to give the director an intellectual analysis: composing place, recreating events, eliciting moral principles, applying them to life in general. They may even recount certain beautiful insights that they have gleaned from commentaries on the text. Yet, they are careful to keep all this revelation on a strictly abstract and theoretical level. They say absolutely nothing of how the Word spoke to their heart or touched their lives through prayer.

Another form of intellectualization which directees employ is that of replacing the manifestation of their true life experiences with descriptions which they have picked up in spiritual reading. "Sometimes it seems that the so called 'interior life' is little more than a web of illusion, spun out of jargon and pious phrases which we have lifted from books and sermons and with which we conceal, rather than reveal what is in us."[5]

Directees may, for example, be exposed to the concept of "the dark night" through study or lectures. Being impressionable, they imagine that they are undergoing this *nada* in the manner described by someone else. Or, when asked by the director to describe their prayer, instead of revealing their personal experience of prayer, they respond with a litany of clichés.

Sometimes directees try to avoid in-depth direction by bringing up controversial theological questions which have little or no bearing on their interior life: for instance, the abortion issue, the ordination of women to the priesthood, papal infallibility. Or, to divert attention they begin theologizing on the morality of nuclear stockpiling, the nature of the Church, the theoretical meaning of communal life or of the vows. Serious spiritual direction presupposes a great

[5]*S. Direction*, p. 31.

deal of very solid and profound theology. Situations arise where the director may need to explain the theological basis for the particular advice which s/he imparts. However, spiritual direction is not theological discourse or reflection. Unnecessary theologizing tends to focus attention on self — be it the director or the directee — and away from God.

On occasion, however, not knowing exactly how to go about revealing themselves, directees begin by asking an apparently abstract question which in reality touches on something of major significance in their life. A wise director must be alert to this. Oftentimes, gently asking them to express their reason for the question will encourage them to bring their personal struggle out into the open.

Sometimes to avoid manifestation of the heart, directees exaggerate an inability to express themselves adequately. They claim that they do not possess eloquence of speech. They insist that they are more feeler than thinker. They try to convince the director that they should, therefore, be excused from even attempting to verbalize the experience of God within them.

Some directees stubbornly insist that they do not know what is going on interiorly. The defense mechanism of "I don't know" is quite contrary to the contemplative stance of "acquiescing in the unknown."[6] The former is a refusal to accept oneself as well as a refusal to reveal oneself. The latter is truly being and becoming oneself in the darkness of faith. The first tends towards isolation and alienation; the second towards solitude and communion. The defense "I don't know" can be indicative of laziness, interior complacency, fear of truth, lack of commitment. The desire to "acquiesce in the unknown" is the result of being sought out by God. It thrusts one ever deeper into the mystery of God. It is the *nada* which is also the *todo* of God.

Certain directees experience deep inner disturbance. Instead of revealing to the director the real source of these difficulties they ascribe their agitation to some other appar-

[6]*C. Prayer*, p. 94.

ently legitimate cause. For example, in discerning a possible call to a more solitary life, a directee begins to discover through lived experience that s/he cannot properly cope with the solitude s/he already has. Instead of admitting this to him/herself (let alone to the director), this directee insists that concern over family problems is causing the unrest. Troublesome family difficulties may indeed exist, but the directee uses these to camouflage his/her inner conflict and scatteredness.

It is normal that some of the above defense mechanisms come into play in the course of ongoing spiritual direction. If we are prudent directors, we remain listening to God, not allowing ourselves to be sidetracked by such behavior. We gently but firmly steer the directee back to the matter of spiritual direction. One approach to accomplish this return is not to respond to these defenses, thereby letting the directee experience their futility. Another approach is to ask a pointed question which brings the discussion back to the issue at hand. At other times, direct confrontation may be necessary. On occasion too, a director may have to bear with these immaturities for quite some time, waiting patiently in a spirit of loving acceptance of the directee. More time may be needed for the directee to develop the confidence and trust necessary to fully reveal him/herself to us.

It happens that after a reasonable passage of time some directees, nonetheless, continue to cling obstinately to these defense mechanisms. Sometimes these defenses become intensified as the director tries to deal with them. In these cases, it is impossible for spiritual direction to continue, since the listening process has been effectively obstructed.

## (2) DIMENSIONS OF OPENNESS

Before they can manifest their heart to the director, directees have to discover first what is in their heart. This discovery can take place only by being alone with themselves — indeed, alone with God in themselves — and being truly at home in this aloneness with God. In the solitude of their heart, directees face themselves as they really are: with no pretense, no masks, no affectation. Having experienced themselves thus, they can then relate something of their experience of God.

Frequently, directees are unable to reveal to us a significant aspect of their interior life simply because they are not yet sufficiently conscious of it. What is important in this case is that they remain as transparent as possible at any given moment. If they are honestly trying to listen, then what they need to see about themselves will be revealed in due course, either through the inspiration of the Spirit from within themselves or from the Spirit working through us as directors.

Besides laying bare as sincerely as possible what is in their heart, directees must do this simply and clearly. They have to tell it like it is. Most of the time they do not have to go into lengthy and complicated explanations. If something can be said in five words, there is no need to take five thousand or even fifty. Verboseness is often a not too subtle attempt to excuse themselves. "We must be perfectly open and simple, without prejudices and without artificial theories about ourselves. We must learn to speak according to our own inner truth, as far as we can perceive it. We must learn to say what we really mean in the depths of our souls, not what we think we are expected to say, not what somebody else has just said. And we must be prepared to take responsibility for our desires, and accept the consequences."[7]

Practically speaking, this suggests that directees not downplay the real difficulties of life or exaggerate difficulty where little or none exists. If a personal relationship is causing interior conflict, they cannot honestly give the impression that all is well. If an unpleasant incident with extenuating circumstances was handled somewhat immaturely, directees must not blow this out of proportion.

[7]*S. Direction*, p. 29.

Pseudo-issues have no place in spiritual direction: Where am I on the ladder of holiness? Exactly what phase of dark night am I undergoing? "It would seem that most of the pseudo-technical questions that seem to require consideration in direction are completely useless and should be forgotten.... The trouble is not that such things are unimportant or unreal but rather that the verbiage that tends to surround them actually gets between the contemplative and reality, between the soul and God."[8] Such questions arise usually from an inordinate desire for empirical certitude which is quite contrary to life in faith. These pseudo-issues stem frequently from deep-rooted pride which seeks the director's affirmation, approval or esteem.

Manifestation of the heart does not imply that directees need to engage in pointless or prolonged digressions. To reveal the history of their souls is one thing. To narrate their whole life story is quite another. If it is necessary to describe an event which took place in their ministry, directees need not bog down the session with related stories. The discipline of sticking to the point is required to facilitate the listening process. Should directees indulge in such tangents and digressions, it is our responsibility as directors to guide the discussion back to the central issues.

Simplicity, honesty and frankness in communicating themselves do not imply that directees have their interior life completely analyzed and categorized. Indeed, any kind of categorization and some forms of self-analysis are antagonistic to true life in faith. Simplicity, honesty and frankness do mean, however, that directees express candidly what they are capable of revealing of their search for God, of their joys and struggles, of their successes and failures, of their inner peace and confusion.

Directees should let their intuition and common sense determine what is important to bring up in spiritual direction. Preoccupation with coherence, logic or polish tends to produce artificiality. They, as well as their directors, must be

[8] *S. Direction*, p. 33.

patient with their often clumsy and disjointed manner of expression.

Directors and directees alike should prepare for their sessions together by listening to God: that is, by contemplative prayer. We may prepare for a class by reviewing our notes. We may prepare for a job interview by detailing a personal resumé. But in spiritual direction, directees do not prepare by preplanning exactly how and what to say to the director. Preoccupation with what should be said leads to unnecessary tension and obstructs their ability to listen to God. "Do not worry about how to speak or what to say. What you are to say will be given when the time comes, because it is not you who will be speaking. The Spirit of your Father will be speaking in you" (*Mt* 10:19-20).

Directees need only listen to God within themselves. Then, having listened, they reveal to the director whatever they intuit as significant in whatever way it comes out.

Sometimes directees intuit something that they must reveal without understanding why. This insight may occur as if out of the blue, unsolicited and unrelated to anything else. Frequently, what directees find themselves disclosing is not at all what they had in mind in the first place. They may make a statement which once voiced leads them to question or to probe more deeply some other aspect of their life. In the very act of verbalizing to us their inner trials and joys with all their underlying hesitations and desires, directees often see for themselves what God's direction is. In these instances, the director may not utter a single word (except possibly: "Hello" and "Good-bye"). Yet, these directees will be quite expressive of their gratitude for all the help we afforded them by remaining silent and listening all the while.

Most of the time, however, directees do receive from us some verbal spiritual direction. If this word is from God, they will experience within themselves an intuitive resonance with the directive — provided, of course, that they are truly listening to God within themselves. Frequently too, we clarify what directees had only vaguely known or expressed.

The question of intuitive resonance can be difficult to discern in the concrete. God is one. Truth is one. Once God's truth is personally experienced, the experience itself is undeniable and unmistakable. Yet this side of the resurrection our perception of God's truth is never pure or whole (1 *Co* 13:12). God may move the director to grasp one aspect of the truth, and the directee another. These two aspects may not be immediately reconcilable. Moreover, because there exists always a strong subjective dimension in every perception of reality — even a perception inspired by God — certain elements of the human weakness of both the director and of the directee are bound to enter into the discernment. Furthermore, each individual's spiritual direction is a personal mystery which unfolds gradually in faith. So it can never be fully grasped. All the loose ends can never, this side of death, be knotted together. Humble listening, continued listening, submissive listening to God eventually brings about enough peace to move forward where we do not see the way.

It happens sometimes that directees have nothing to say going into a scheduled meeting with their director. Unless circumstances warrant otherwise, they should still keep the appointment. We may well have something to say, even though they do not. Conversely, directees may be very anxious to receive specific spiritual direction, while we have nothing at all to say. The Spirit himself moves both the director and the directee regarding what, when and how to speak. We must each wait patiently for the Spirit's movement in the other.

Directees reveal themselves not only by words but also through their whole manner of being.

Body language can reveal something of the intensity and depth of their life in faith as well as of their weaknesses and struggles. Oftentimes the very manner in which a particular word is spoken indicates that something vital is being withheld, possibly out of fear or embarrassment. Facial expressions — the eyes in particular — bespeak relaxation or tension, sociability or isolation, peace or anxiety, warmth or aloofness.

On the one hand, silence between the director and the directee may be expressive of the tranquility produced by abiding together in mystery. Silence can indicate wonder at God's ways. It can express peaceful acceptance of truth. On the other hand, silence can be ominously filled with pain, anger, hostility or sullenness. It can indicate an inability on the part of directees to express themselves as well as an attempt to manipulate us by trying to force us to speak when the Spirit is silent.

## (3) Personal Salvation History

Particularly if a relationship promises to be of long duration, directors should invite directees to give an account of their personal salvation history. This recounting of their spiritual genesis is a sharing with us of how they have perceived God's transforming and consuming love operative within themselves and through the events of their lives.

The history of their souls greatly aids us in discerning how their lives have unfolded thus far. The more deeply we know their salvation history, the better prepared we are to listen with them in the present. Knowledge of their spiritual genesis increases our ability to perceive their current direction. Moreover, in light of their overall salvation history we may be able to interpret more accurately the significance of a certain event or of an interior change presently occurring.

Initially, the account of their salvation history may consist in a broad overview. Later, however, in the course of spiritual direction certain aspects of the life story of these directees may have to be explored in greater depth. The purpose of this exploration would be to discover more fully the meaningfulness of certain past experiences or to help resolve a present and related area of difficulty.

We can help directees reflect on their salvation history by identifying the critical thresholds in their spiritual genesis. These thresholds correspond usually to the normal phases and passages of growing up and of growing old. We can help directees appreciate the constant love and fidelity of God on their behalf throughout the entirety of their lives. Through our challenges and observations regarding their past, directees can attain better self-understanding and self-acceptance in the present.

*Chapter 6*

# Basic Principles for Listening

In order to respond properly to the directee's manifestation of the heart and to safeguard the quality of the listening process, directors follow certain fundamental principles.

## A. The Spiritual Director is an Instrument of God

As spiritual directors we operate first, foremost and always from the premise that God is the only director of any person. We are consequently no more than God's instruments, albeit free instruments, in the process of spiritual direction.

That the director is but an instrument of God is stressed by all the great spiritual masters. The following are a few testimonies:

"Let such guides of souls recall that the principal agent, guide and mover of souls....is not the director, but the Holy Spirit....They are themselves only instruments to guide souls in the way of perfection by faith and by the law of God according to the spirit that God is giving each one."[1]

[1] *Flame*, 3, 46.

"God alone is our only master and director; and creatures, when he is pleased to use them, are only his instruments. So that all other teachers whatsoever...are no further nor otherwise to be followed or hearkened to, than as they are subordinate and conformable to the internal directions and inspirations of God's Holy Spirit, or as God invites, instructs, and moves us to have recourse unto them."[2]

[The director's guidance] "is, in reality, nothing more than a way of leading us to see and obey our real Director — the Holy Spirit, hidden in the depths of our soul. We must never forget that in reality we are not directed and taught by men, and that if we need human 'direction' it is only because we cannot, without man's help, come into contact with that 'unction (of the Spirit) which teaches us all things (1 *Jn* 2:20).'"[3]

God himself is the primary cause of spiritual direction. This function is attributed frequently to the person of the Holy Spirit. Depending on one's point of view, the same can be said equally of Christ or of the Father.

As in all cases of instrumental causality, both the primary cause and the instrumental cause concur to produce a common effect. Each leaves its own mark on the effect, but the primary always remains primary while the instrumental remains instrumental.

Biblical inspiration is a convenient analogue to spiritual direction in this respect. Through inspiration God moves a person to write. Both are the author of a given scriptural passage. Both produce a common effect, yet each imparts his own quality to the work. There is only one Gospel of Jesus Christ, but it is according to Matthew, Mark, Luke and John. Paul's letters to the Thessalonians and Corinthians are both the word of God and the word of Paul, yet they remain primarily God's word which he uses however he wills. Paul intended his letters for particular churches. God

[2]*H. Wisdom*, p. 41.
[3]*S. Direction*, p. 30.

intends them for humankind. Paul was fiery and impetuous. God used those qualities. Paul believed that the parousia was imminent. God revealed his truth about the second coming in spite of Paul's mistaken assumption. Paul held narrow personal views about woman's place in society. That fact did not impede God in the least.

Similarly, God uses the whole personality of the director to impart spiritual direction to a directee. Gifts, knowledge, experience, personal prayer life, as well as weaknesses, biases, inexperience, all come into play. Even our particular manner of expression is utilized. Our very effort to listen to God and to search for him is integral to our collaboration with the Spirit in the spiritual regeneration of the directee. Nonetheless, God's word is distinguishable from the director's even though God's word comes through the director.

As instruments of the Spirit, we are concerned principally with fostering in directees maximum receptivity to God's transforming and purifying love. Under the guidance of the Spirit, we assist directees to discern the obstacles which block or slow down the growth of Christ within them. We afford them appropriate advice or encouragement as well.

It is our responsibility to prepare in directees a way for the Lord. We are to guide them into detachment from everything created, whether spiritual or material so that they can journey with faith, hope and love as their only support. "Let those who guide...be content with disposing the soul according to evangelical perfection which is detachment and emptiness of sense and spirit. Let them not seek to go beyond this in building up the soul, because that work belongs only to the Father.... Your work is the preparation of the soul. It is the work of God to direct its way (*Pr* 16:1, 9)....that is, to direct it to supernatural blessings by ways and in manners that neither you nor the soul can understand."[4]

Like John the Baptizer, we help directees discover God who is intimately present, yet often unrecognized: "There stands in your midst — unknown to you — One who is

---

[4]*Flame*, 3, 47. See *Receptivity*, pp. 17-53, 114-120.

coming.... Behold, the Lamb of God!.... It was to reveal him that I have come" (*Jn* 1:26-31). Having thus pointed directees beyond themselves to God, we stand back entrusting them entirely to him.

## B. The Director is Abandoned to God in Faith.

We can be effective instruments of the Spirit only if we are completely surrendered to God in faith. Since we are concerned solely with discerning the mysterious will of the Father for each directee, we have to be fully at the disposal of God. We are truly servants of the mystery of Christ who came not to do his own will, but the will of the One who sent him (*Jn* 4:34).

Our abandonment to God must be to the point of complete detachment from all desire to give directees any particular directive or insight as well as from any desire for immediate and tangible solutions to difficulties. Nor may we demand from God specific graces which we imagine will immediately perfect our directees. To demand this of God would be presumptuous. It would be to expect some-*thing*. God calls us into this relationship not to speculate on what directees need, but rather to listen to him revealing their needs. We therefore wait on God in silent expectancy, humbly accepting either the presence or the absence of any inspiration from him and open to any way that he chooses to make his direction known.

## C. A Spiritual Direction Exists Already Within the Directee

God loves all his creation. "God looked at all that he had made, and saw that it was indeed very good" (*Gn* 1:31). Moreover, "God so loved the world that he gave his only begotten Son" (*Jn* 3:16).

The intimacy and the fidelity of God's love are especially striking in reference to the creation of the human person: "I betroth you to myself forever. I betroth you with integrity and justice, with tenderness and love. I betroth you to myself with faithfulness and you will come to know Yahweh" (*Ho* 2:21-22). "I have called you by name. You are mine.... You are precious in my eyes...and I love you"(*Is* 43: 1, 4). "I have loved you with an everlasting love" (*Jr* 31:3). So intimate is God's love that he actually dwells within each person (*Jn* 15:5).

No two persons experience the love of God in exactly the same manner. He loves each of us infinitely and personally. God does not love one more and another less. Yet, his love is so personalized that we each experience it differently. "There are many rooms in my Father's house" (*Jn* 14:2). Thus, the specific way a person is transformed and purified is unique by virtue of God's singular love for him/her. "It was you who created my inmost self, and put me together in my mother's womb. For all these wonders, I thank you; for the wonder of myself, for the wonder of your works" (*Ps* 139:13-14).

Who and how we are to become — that is, our personhood and our vocation — are given to us by God in one simultaneous act. "Before I formed you in the womb, I knew you. Before you came to birth I consecrated you. I sent you forth" (*Jr* 1:5). Within our inmost being God implants his call. That call attains its full actualization only in our transformation in him through death. The Spirit directs us from within throughout the entirety of the process of our divinization.

Consequently, the direction which a directee is seeking to discover is already within him/herself. "My word is very near to you. Indeed, it is in your mouth and within your heart. Therefore, obey it." (*Dt* 30:14). The director and the directee have only to discern the direction as it emerges from within the directee.

This truth has far-reaching implications. Never can we approach directees with a priori ways or with predetermined solutions. We guide according to the manner and the spirit whereby God leads each one. We assist directees to find their own proper way to the Father. What is appropriate for one may be quite inappropriate for another.

St. John of the Cross advises: "The whole concern of the director should be not to accommodate souls to his own way or to what suits him. Rather he ought to see if he can discern the particular way along which God is leading them. If he cannot discern the way proper to each, he should leave them alone and not disturb them."[5]

Thus we need the flexibility and openness to accept each directee as s/he is — a unique individual infinitely loved by God. We cannot categorize or classify any person according to "case" or "problem." Nor should we ever compare one person with another.

The Spirit uses us in diverse ways to open directees to God's direction within them. Sometimes he leads us to use painful means: correction, firmness, confrontation. At other times the Spirit calls forth gentleness, encouragement, affirmation. All ways must proceed equally from love.

Quite frequently, we are called to help directees identify and dispel illusions. In fact, most of the effort exerted in spiritual direction addresses precisely this need. The unmasking of illusions consists principally in helping directees un-know the mistaken assumptions which they entertain regarding God, self, prayer, love, sin, etc. The discovery of who God is not, of who they are not, of what prayer, love, sin, etc. are not, is for directees an invaluable dimension of the discovery of their inner direction.

In unmasking illusions, the director challenges directees at the beckoning of the Spirit. This challenge consists often in asking directees pointed questions with respect to their attitudes, outlook on life, relationships with God and others. Through our challenge, the Spirit draws directees out of their complacency and egocentricity in order to participate more fully in the freedom of God.

We are also to help directees recognize and formulate their own questions properly. To identify the real issues we have to pierce through the confusion and turmoil of the directees' sometimes jumbled thoughts and feelings. We cannot expect a precise answer to these questions, however. Rather, the mere posing of a question correctly usually suffices to dispose directees to be more open to whatever truth the Spirit wants to reveal therein.

The distinction between spiritual direction and psychological counseling is generally considered to be this: Counseling is essentially nondirective and client-oriented. Spiritual direction, on the other hand, is basically directive and oriented towards the moral and ethical behavior of the directee. This attitude may indeed reflect widespread practice in certain milieus. However, that praxis is not representative of spiritual direction in the deeper sense which we have been describing.

In this deeper sense, spiritual direction is even more nondirective than counseling because the directee's spiritual direction is already within him/ her. The director's prime responsibility is to facilitate the bringing into consciousness of what already is. The director does not give spiritual direction. S/ he discerns it. Moreover, spiritual direction in this sense is oriented towards neither the client nor ethical behavior as such. It is God-oriented pure and simple.

### D. The Director Imparts Guidance Only When Moved Interiorly by the Spirit to Do So.

Since we are instruments of the Spirit, any word spoken to the directee must emerge out of our own silent listening to God. Only in this way can God communicate through us as Jesus promised: "It is not you who will be speaking. The Spirit of your Father will be speaking in you" (*Mt* 10:20). "Whoever listens to you listens to me" (*Lk* 10:16).

This is indeed a crucial principle in spiritual direction. Speak only when prompted interiorly to do so. Jesus himself is the prime example: "The words which I speak to you are not from me. They are the words of the Father abiding in me" (*Jn* 14:10).

We can never presume to direct another on personal initiative alone. We cannot speak just because the directee expects us to do so or hopes that we will. When nothing is forthcoming, we are to rest in nothing (*nada*): doing nothing, saying nothing. If we do not understand what God is indicating, we have to wait with patience. If we do not see the way, we are not to pretend that we do. We undergo this experience of our poverty in faith and in mystery. We may be easily tempted on these occasions to act out of a desire to appear holy or competent or even out of a desire to feel in control of the situation. *Nada* can also be from God, and it plays a very important role in God's direction of the directee.

Neither should we become preoccupied with what to say or how to say it. Undue concern with such matters arises from a tendency to be self-reliant and self-sufficient. We have to approach the directee in a spirit of complete abandonment to God. "Do not worry about how to speak or what to say. What you are to say will be given when the time comes, because it is not you who will be speaking. The Spirit of your Father will be speaking in you" (*Mt* 10:19-20).

Directing only when moved interiorly in no way implies affectation. It has nothing to do with somberness, false piety or mimicking the style of another director whom we admire. If such were indeed the case, this behavior would give rise to stress and awkwardness within us. This in turn would lead the directee to be ill at ease. Furthermore, such pretence would obstruct the direction process, since we become so engaged in playing a role that we are no longer able to listen.

On the contrary, the ability to direct only when prompted interiorly presupposes that we are comfortable in being with another person without feeling compelled to say or to do anything. They also serve who just wait. True spiritual direction emerges in an atmosphere which is relaxed and natural. A good director possesses much self-discipline and interior leisure.

As essential as this principle is in spiritual direction, it can be difficult to implement. Putting it into practice requires a very personal and concrete response to Jesus's invitation: "If anyone wishes to come after me, let him deny himself and take up his cross daily and follow me" (*Lk* 9:23). To follow the Spirit's initiative entails a profound experience of our personal helplessness, poverty and utter dependence upon God.

Instead of waiting to guide the directee when and as moved by the Spirit, we easily let a myriad of human weaknesses get to us. For example, when the Spirit is silent we may feel obliged to say something out of a desire for approval or as a misguided way of consoling an impatient directee. God may actually need our corresponding silence to bring about what he wants to accomplish in the directee.

Remaining silent when so moved by the Spirit does not imply aloofness, coldness or distance towards the directee. On the contrary, it is an intense way of being with another in the manner which God wishes at that time. As such, silence is a true expression of love and caring.

Sometimes too the reverse tendency occurs. Instead of wanting to speak when we should remain silent, we would prefer to be silent when we should speak up. For instance, we may be moved interiorly to make an unpleasant observation, to raise a thorny question or even to use direct confrontation. Yet, rather than acting on this inspiration we say nothing out of fear of being mistaken, of hurting the directee or of personal rejection. Such taciturnity has nothing at all to do with true silence. On the contrary, it is to succumb to inner noise and clutteredness.

We may be tempted also to avoid the issue when directees begin to disclose something in their life which has bearing on an unresolved area in our own life. Suppose a directee begins to perceive a call to spend more time each day in solitary prayer. If we are refusing to respond to a similar call in our life, we may brush the subject aside, telling the directee that length of time is not important, that it is best to pray only when one feels like it, or that the extra time could be better used for ministerial activity.

By its very nature, the principle of directing only when moved necessarily excludes chitchat while listening to God within the directee. At the beginning of an encounter, a person may need a little casual conversation in order to feel at ease. Once serious spiritual direction has begun, however, the director and the directee should refrain from casual remarks, jokes, frivolous comments, superficial conversation. All this tends to obstruct the listening process by misplacing the reason for coming together in the first place. Even in instances where some casual conversation is initially helpful, it should be principally our listening presence and silent manner of being that most effectively radiate love, gentleness, acceptance and receptivity toward the directee. In some cases, the director and the directee may be personal friends or co-workers. Friendly conversations or discussions related to work are of course in order. But they should take place outside the context of spiritual direction.

In order to facilitate openness to the Spirit in spiritual direction, directors refrain also from unneccessary theoretical discussions, from argumentation over controversial issues and from petty wrangling over terminology. When conflicts arise between the director and directee, such defense mechanisms become especially tempting.

"In the presence of God, there is to be no wrangling over words. All this ever achieves is the destruction of those who are listening...Shun profane, empty chatter since this only leads further and further away from true religion. Talk of this kind corrodes like gangrene.... Avoid foolish and stupid speculations, knowing that they only give rise to quarrels. A servant of the Lord is not to quarrel, but must be gentle towards everyone, a good teacher and patient" (2 *Tm* 2:14-17, 23-24).

## E. The Director Relies on Divine Wisdom

In the course of the relationship between director and directee there will be a time for everything: "A time for birthing and a time for dying; a time for planting and a time for uprooting." A time for hurting "and a time for healing; a time for tearing down and a time for rebuilding. A time for tears and a time for laughter; a time for embracing and a time to refrain from embracing. A time for searching and a time for abandoning; a time for keeping and a time for letting go.... A time for remaining silent and a time for speaking" (*Qo* 3:1-8).

How then are we to know the appropriate time? How do we recognize the interior movement to guide a directee in a particular way?

Certainly, as thorough a knowledge as possible of ascetical-mystical theology and competency with the principles of discernment cannot be overstressed. Yet, in actual spiritual direction directors rely principally and immediately on divine wisdom.

In listening to God within ourselves and within the directee we receive the wisdom to know the appropriate direction as well as the proper time and manner to express it. The experience of love's relentless searching for God brings the listening person quickly to the grace of discernment. We do not set out to attain this grace. There is nothing that we can do, strictly speaking, to acquire it. We receive from God the ability to discern as we remain lovingly attentive to him. Discernment flows out of God's loving interchange with us and subtly impresses itself upon our consciousness. It is like opening our eyes, and there it is. We are awakened to it.

The awareness which results from this intuitive, loving communion with God is called "divine wisdom." It is divine because it is directly and immediately from God. It is wisdom because it is loving knowledge. It is the kind of knowledge which is experienced in love and results from love (in contradistinction to logic, reasoning, analysis, etc.).

Divine wisdom is learning in love. The author of *The Cloud of Unknowing* describes the mystery thus:

"If you wish to be off quickly and unerringly on your spiritual journey, one thing suffices and nothing more: God alive in your mind and active in your heart, gently arousing you to everlasting love. Yes, this is God's way to God and it will not fail you.... This very love you experience tells you unerringly when to speak and when to be silent. It will guide you discreetly and without error in everything. It will enlighten you in secret with great and surpassing discretion, teaching you when to begin and when to leave off.... Try with God's grace then to abide continually in the work of love for I assure you ... this love will immediately take the initiative and gently prod you to know and to do whatever is necessary."[6]

So effective is this prodding of love that we cannot resist it indefinitely. We may attempt to deny it, run from it, argue with it, but we cannot succeed. Divine wisdom pursues us relentlessly. We experience it as something we must say or do regardless of personal cost and possible consequences. Eventually, we experience a veritable inability to do other than freely act on this wisdom: "If you fail to respond," this love "will smite you and grievously wound your heart, leaving you no peace until you act. Likewise, if you are speaking ... and it were more helpful for you to be silent ... this love will again prod you relentlessly until you do it."[7]


## F. The Director Never Makes Decisions for the Directee.

This principle goes without saying: The director never assumes personal responsibility for the directee's life. We advise, instruct, correct; confirm, encourage, affirm; even give specific directives at times. However, the directee always retains full personal responsibility for his/her decisions and choices. The purpose of spiritual direction is to help directees help themselves be helped by God. Rather than fostering dependency, we seek to assist the directee in becoming more mature, responsible and free.

Spiritual direction should leave the directee an emancipated pilgrim.


[6]*A Pistle of Discrecioun of Stirings,* in *Contemplative Review* 10 (1, 1977) 17-18.

[7]*Ibidem.*

*Chapter 7*

# Divine Wisdom

Spiritual direction is a listening. A spiritual direction is discerned through listening. This listening is a loving, receptive attentiveness to God in sincere detachment from all desire to see, t  hear, to know, to feel or to control anything at all. As this detached listening intensifies, there emerges a certain kind of seeing and knowing which are permeated with the perception of God himself. This seeing and knowing arise intuitively from within both the director and the directee. This is wisdom: divine wisdom.

## A. The Hebrew hakmah

In the Old Testament, the evolution of the notion of wisdom is long and varied, yet through all these transmutations, a single word dominates: *hakmah*, which is rendered into Greek by *sophia*.

Initially, the wise person was one skilled in practical matters. Wisdom denoted an advanced degree of dexterity in one's daily work as well as an accomplished shrewdness in one's judgments. Thus, Solomon (before his decline) was the paragon of wisdom in that his incomparable managerial and administrative skills derived from Hebrew tradition, personal experience and divine gift. Any wise person in Israel was highly disciplined, tried and proven.

With time and deeper reflection, the notion of wisdom evolved beyond the sphere of human practicality. Out of Judaism's encounter with Hellenism emerged the Israelite perception of wisdom's eternal origin. Speaking in the first person, wisdom expresses her everlasting perfection:

> "Yahweh brought me forth before the oldest of his works. From eternity I was fashioned; from the beginning , before the world began." (*Pr* 8:22-23)

The purpose and order discernible in the universe are the effects of divine wisdom. She (both *hakmah* and *sophia* are feminine) is a cosmic, creative principle in the design of God:

> "When Yahweh established the heavens, I was there... When he laid the foundation of the earth, I was with him. I was the craftsman at his side delighting him day after day, as one continuously rejoicing in his presence." (*Pr* 8:27-30)

A further threshold was crossed when wisdom became perceived as a person: a hypostasis. Wisdom proceeds from the mouth of God (*Si* 24:3). She is a breath of the power of the Most High, a pure emanation of the glory of the Almighty, a reflection of eternal light, an image of God's loving kindness (*Ws* 7:25-26). Wisdom initiates us into the knowledge of the mysteries of God. She discerns his works. The qualities of wisdom are manifold:

> "She comprises an intelligent, holy, unique spirit. Wisdom is diversified, subtle, active. She is unsullied, lucid, invulnerable; always benevolent, sharp, irresistible.
>
> Wisdom is beneficent, loving, steadfast; dependable and unperturbed.

> She can do anything, survive anything, penetrate
> anything.
> Wisdom is the most wise, the most single-hearted, the
> most subtle of spirits.
> She is quicker to move than any motion.
> Wisdom is so pure that she pervades and permeates all
> things." (*Ws* 7:22-24)

The Hebrews accepted eagerly the unfolding revelation of divine wisdom. Their understanding of wisdom as a creative, cosmic principle and as a mysterious personal extension of God himself made possible for them the recognition and the acceptance of the fact that other nations as well possessed truth. Because wisdom was inherently manifest in all creation, she was therefore accessible to all peoples.

Even the pristine notion of wisdom as practical skill was later embraced in a more mature manner, for astuteness and dexterity were perceived as participations in God's own wisdom. Wisdom's influence was thus operative throughout every aspect of life — from the most sublime to the most earthy, from the most mysterious to the most concrete.

Israel considered itself uniquely privileged among all nations with regard to divine wisdom. For God had commanded *hakmah*: "Pitch your tent in Jacob, make Israel your inheritance" (*Si* 24:13). Wisdom thus coincides with divine revelation. She is embodied preeminently in the Torah (*Si* 24:23-34).

Several striking characteristics of wisdom are revealed in the Old Testament:

(1) First and foremost, *hakmah* pertains to the mystery of God himself: "All wisdom is from the Lord. She is his forever" (*Si* 1:1). He is her author, her animator, her sole reason for being.

Although traces of wisdom are found everywhere, nowhere in the cosmos can wisdom be grasped in herself. God alone knows her and possesses her. Job reflects: Tell me, "Where does wisdom come from? Where is her dwelling place? The road to wisdom is still unknown to us.... She transcends the knowledge of every living being.... God alone has traced her path and knows her abode" (*Jb* 28:12-23).

(2) God makes us participators in his wisdom. She is his free gift to us. "God himself has created her, looked on her and assessed her. He poured her out on all his works. She is his gift to all humankind" (*Si* 1:9-10). "Yahweh is the giver of wisdom. From his mouth issue forth knowledge and discernment" (*Pr* 2:6).

Solomon prayerfully recognized wisdom as being inherently Yahweh's. Knowing that he could not master wisdom on his own, Solomon confessed: "I turned to the Lord and entreated him with all my heart..., 'grant me wisdom'" (*Ws* 8:21, 9:4). And God gave him "a listening heart" (1 *Kg* 3:9).

(3) The gift of wisdom is received from God within our inmost being: "In each generation she passes into holy souls. She makes them friends of God and prophets, for God loves only the one who lives by wisdom" (*Ws* 7:27-28).

(4) God imparts wisdom only to those who respond faithfully to his initiative: "He conveys her to those who love him" (*Si* 1:10). "God bestows wisdom, knowledge and happiness on the person who delights him" (*Qo* 2:26).

In the Old Testament, then, wisdom denotes not only skillfulness and astuteness in practical matters, but especially an intuitive knowledge and a divinely bestowed discernment in the affairs of God. Wisdom cannot be achieved or merited. She is shared freely with those who respond faithfully to the Lord's love. Divine wisdom, therefore, arises out of God's incomparable love for a person as well as out of his/her loving response to the Lord.

## B. *The New Testament* sophia

While it encompasses all the above qualities, the New Testament revelation concerning divine wisdom surpasses infinitely the Hebraic *hakmah*. The personification of wisdom reaches its apex in the person and mission of the Word made flesh (*Jn* 1:14).

The Hebraic view of wisdom as the Law is also super-ceded in the New Testament. The Synoptics portray Jesus as the Wisdom of God in passages which stress his fulfillment and transcendence of the Law (e.g., *Mt* 5:17-18; *Lk* 4:21). But it is Paul who is most explicit with regard to wisdom. He contrasts eloquently divine wisdom with human wisdom (1 *Co* 1:17-2:16). He applies wisdom directly to each person of the Trinity: "Glory be to God [the Father] who alone is wisdom" (*Rm* 16:27). "May the Father of glory grant you the Spirit of wisdom" (*Eph* 1:17). Jesus himself — most especially Christ crucified — is revealed as *the* Wisdom of the Father (1 *Co* 1:24, 30). The incarnate and resurrected Word is "the wisdom that God predestined for our glory before the ages began" (1 *Co* 2:7). In Christ Jesus we find made visible the infinite treasures of God's hidden wisdom (*Col* 2:3).

## C. Wisdom in Spiritual Direction

In reference to the spiritual life, wisdom is loving knowl-edge. It is the kind of knowledge which flows from interper-sonal communion with God and is directed towards transforming union with him in love. St. John of the Cross has several expressions to render wisdom in this sense: general, loving, dark, peaceful knowledge; obscure and unspecified knowledge; loving, peaceful, simple knowledge; secret knowledge.[1]

This intuitive knowledge is of God in the sense that it is from him and to him, not just about him. It is to know God in himself inasmuch as we are humanly capable in this life. Divine wisdom is the result of direct communion with God, without passing through any created medium. It is to expe-rience in love that which most uniquely constitutes God as God.

---

[1] *Ascent*, II, 13-15; II, 10, 4; *Night*, I, 10, 4; *Flame*, 3, 34; *Canticle*, 27, 5.

Who is God? God is Father, Son and Spirit. What is God? "God is Spirit" (*Jn* 4:24). "God is Light" (1 *Jn* 1:5). "God is Love" (1 *Jn* 4:8).

Divine wisdom results from the experience of that which is deepest, most mysterious and loving in Father, Son and Spirit. We perceive this wisdom as dark, obscure, elusive, ineffable, although it is in itself pure light. This loving knowledge guides us beyond knowing in its usual sense in order to know God by unknowing. Thus, wisdom is not reasoning, nor is it part of the reasoning process. We may receive wisdom without even adverting directly to the fact.

Integral to divine wisdom is the ever deepening awareness of both the immanence and the transcendence of God. Because our experience of God remains in mystery, we necessarily pass through an unknowing of all that we had previously conceived him to be. We realize that however provident, loving, merciful we have known him, no concept or image adequately expresses him as he is in himself. While there is a certain truth in our conceptualizations of God, he is never exactly who or what we say he is. This is so because he is always infinitely more. The mystical experience of this truth leaves us stammering, while referring to God as "an I-don't-know-what."[2]

We receive this loving knowledge in faith without going through any process of reasoning, analyzing or synthesizing. In fact, because wisdom at this depth does not consist in anything specific or precise, we may not even be aware of having received it: For, "it is at times so subtle and delicate... that we do not perceive it or feel it even though we are engaged in it."[3] This is especially the case when divine wisdom is in itself most pure, simple and spiritual, as well as when we ourselves are most purified of particular kinds of knowledge with which the understanding or senses might be preoccupied.

---

[2] *Un no-sé-qué* (*Canticle*. 7. 10); poem *Por toda la hermosura* (the seventh line of every stanza). See *Contemplation*, pp. 36-52.

[3] *Ascent*, II, 14, 8; see *Night*, II, 8, 1-5.

Most of the time divine wisdom remains so profound and mysterious that we do not experience more than a general, intuitive consciousness of its presence. This is so because our cognitive powers in this mortal life cannot penetrate or grasp that degree of simplicity. Our minds are really very cluttered. Yet, when it is helpful to our proper response to his grace, God causes his wisdom in us to become concretized so that we can comprehend some specific aspect of it. This concretization of divine wisdom transpires always in faith. It is never reducible to the precision or clarity of empirical certitude. For example, the unswerving commitment that we experience towards our vocation is never on the same plane as a mathematical equation.

In spiritual direction both the director and the directee receive some divine wisdom from their listening to God. The more loving the listening, the purer the wisdom. Then, when the interior disposition is ripe, the Spirit grants also to both of them some particular knowledge or insight. It is especially this concretization of wisdom which enables the director to guide directees. It empowers directees as well to discern what spiritual direction is compatible with their interior thrust. This concrete knowledge and insight facilitate the directee's voluntary entry into greater communion with God. They deepen also his/her participation in the general, loving knowledge of God and of his creation.

This participation in God's wisdom which we receive as directors pertains to what St. Paul calls "prophecy" and "discernment of spirits" (1 *Co* 12:10). Properly understood, these gifts enable us to see reality as God sees it and to distinguish in complex situations what is truly of God and what is not. They permit us to appreciate what God has brought forth in directees, what he is accomplishing currently in them and where he intends to lead them.

St. John of the Cross furnishes some helpful insight into the process by which the Spirit concretizes divine wisdom and discernment for us.[4] Applying these suggestions specifi-

---

[4]*Ascent*, II, 26, 11-18. The same for all quotations unless otherwise identified in the remainder of this chapter.

cally to spiritual direction, we have a description of the manner in which the director receives the wisdom necessary to guide a directee.

(1) The reception of this particular knowledge "includes the awareness of the truth of things in themselves as well as an understanding of events and happenings which occur in our lives."

Wisdom thus provides the spiritual insight necessary to distinguish sincerity from insincerity, honesty from dishonesty, reality from illusion. It enables us to pierce through ambiguities and confusion in order to perceive God as he is incarnating himself in the person and life of the directee. Divine wisdom permits us to transcend appearances and defenses in order to penetrate the heart. Wisdom disposes us to recognize God transparent within the directee.

"When the soul receives these truths, they are so embedded within its interior ... that if someone were to attempt to convince it of the opposite, the soul would be unable to give its consent, even if it tried to force itself to do so."

Once we perceive this wisdom, we are unable to do other than abide by it. Divine wisdom demands fidelity to its truth. To be true to ourselves and to God, we cannot go against this conviction and remain interiorly at peace.

Moreover, this concretization of divine wisdom "comes to the soul passively without it doing anything." It is entirely from God himself. To do anything, in the sense of initiating on our own some form of rational analysis or logical synthesis, would only impede God's direction of the directee and frustrate the spiritual direction process. We have only to listen to God, search for him, wait on him, and receive in faith whatever God wants to reveal when and as he deems fit. But God does not always reveal to the same director everything he wants a given directee to know for his/her proper direction. Therefore, we should not be surprised or discouraged if God limits our participation in his divine wisdom.

(2) The Mystical Doctor pinpoints the source of divine wisdom:

"Our spirit knows ... by means of the Spirit who presents truth to it." "God infuses" wisdom "in souls by supernatural means whenever he wishes." "They perceive" this knowledge "through their already enlightened and purified spirits."

God himself, in the person of the Holy Spirit, is the source of divine wisdom, be it general or particular. We in turn perceive this wisdom within our own spirits to the extent that we are being transformed in God, and can say in truth: "I live, now no longer I, but Christ lives in me" (*Ga* 2:20).

Thus, wisdom does not come from outside us. It is from God abiding in the inmost depths of our being that wisdom is received. From our loving communion with the indwelling Father, Son and Spirit, wisdom emerges.

Basically then, we allow the Spirit within us to enlighten our consciousness with the wisdom to discern God within the directee. We dispose ourselves to receive this wisdom by listening to God, by searching for him, by waiting on him. In a word, we become most disposed to divine wisdom by contemplation.[5]

(3) How does divine wisdom operate within the director? How does the director give spiritual direction in and through wisdom?

Although we do not normally know what is inside another, we can arrive at this understanding through two means: (1) directly by interior enlightenment, and (2) indirectly by certain signs such as body language.

God may awaken our consciousness to truth directly from within, without using any medium. Truth dawns on us. An insight seems to come out of the blue. "It may happen that while one is thinking of something else, a keen understanding ... will be received in one's spirit: a perception far clearer than what could be conveyed through words." Without being in any way informed from the outside, we may intuit a specific difficulty in the directee's life. An insight

---

[5]See *Contemplation*, pp. 36-43.

which we had not even remotely considered with respect to the directee will spontaneously present itself.

Once this wisdom is received and rendered conscious, usually we perceive certain signs in the directee which confirm it. On rare occasion, we may recognize in faith that a certain insight is from God, and yet be unable to pinpoint any external signs of its authenticity.

More often than not, however, God uses a combination of interacting external signs and interior inspiration to awaken in us the appropriate spiritual direction for the directee. Frequently, the reading of the exterior signs precedes the awareness of more particular interior enlightenment. This is so, since in general we recognize more readily the Spirit outside —communicating through the senses — than the Spirit inside "teaching spiritual things spiritually" (1 *Co* 2:13). For this reason as well, certain discernments are quite lengthy. We may pick up all kinds of bits and pieces from the directee trying to manifest his/her heart. But until God grants the interior inspiration which weaves them together, the bits and pieces of insight remain just so many dangling threads.

The signs and indications of God's will are generally contained within the more ordinary aspects of the directee's life: personal relationships, praying habits, ministry, body language, etc. These signs run the gamut from being very subtle to decidedly obvious. We may perceive them intuitively or as the result of careful reasoning: thinking through the situation, pondering all angles, debating pros and cons. Usually, a whole complex of influences and means converge and interact in order for a single directive or decision to emerge.

(4) The question arises: Does the gift of wisdom ensure that the director will be capable of discerning in every instance?

The response should be obvious: The ability to discern depends entirely on God's will.

In granting us his wisdom, God does not necessarily want it to become concretized in every instance. Why not? That is the Father's business (*Lk* 2:49). Usually though, in these cases God is inviting both the director and the directee to a more purified abandonment and to a deeper search in faith.

Thus, an insight or a word is not always forthcoming when the director would expect it or want it. God grants wisdom in his time and in his way. At any point along the discernment process, God for his own mysterious reasons may withhold a concretization of wisdom. As painful and as perplexing as this may be for those involved, this apparent lack of direction may indeed be the Spirit's way of directing both the director and the directee towards God.

(5) Generally then, how reliable is the spiritual director's ability to discern?

"Although these spiritual persons may sometimes be mistaken ... most often they are correct."

No director is infallible. Even a very competent director can find it quite difficult to help a certain directee listen to God. We may fail to perceive what the directee is trying to express or completely misread the signs. We can minimize a serious difficulty or imagine obstacles where none in fact exists. We may on occasion even give advice that is inappropriate or detrimental to the directee's spiritual growth.

In such instances we should first of all accept the mistake, and if circumstances permit, correct it. Beyond this, however, we must trust that God in his providence will correct any and all deformation or misdirection that may have occurred. After all, God does convert everything into good for those who love him (*Rm* 8:28).

Nevertheless, while truly spiritual directors can be mistaken in their discernment, most often they are correct to the extent that God wishes to use them. Thus, even at the risk of occasionally misinterpreting the signs, we must be always courageous enough to speak what we believe to be the truth.

(6) What ought to be the interior attitude of the director towards this participation in divine wisdom?

John of the Cross responds: "Such knowledge, whether it be of God or not, can be of little help to the progress of the soul on its journey to God if the soul tries to cling to it." Both the director and the directee "must remain detached from such knowledge."

When we perceive a specific insight, whether it be from God, psychology or reason — whatever the source or means — our basic attitude must be that of detached faith. The attempt to grasp wisdom is like trying to grasp air. It always eludes us. As soon as we cling to some particular knowledge, we lose the receptivity necessary to listen to God within ourselves as well as within the directee. Attachment to our own ways and perceptions, together with pride in our ability to discern, results inevitably in spiritual blindness.

A spirit of detachment is required for at least two reasons: *First*, any specific direction is necessarily relative. Discernment usually involves a long process of searching through many possibilities before God's direction emerges. Therefore, while a given directive may be quite valid at one phase in the process, it may have to be changed later or discarded altogether as the directee matures and as God's will becomes more manifest. It is like gradually abandoning discursive prayer as one is being drawn increasingly into contemplation.[6]

*Second*, the director can never be absolutely sure that a particular directive is entirely from God. We have to remain always open to the possibility that what we think is divine wisdom may be a mistaken judgment arising from our own human limitations or from unresolved weaknesses and conflicts within ourselves. While we must act as best we can on our insights, we can never cease testing them: "It is not every spirit that you can trust. Test them to see if they are from God" (1 *Jn* 4:1).

Both the director and the directee should be detached also from any attempt to cling to an authentic directive as a way of evading the *nada*, the night or the dread inherent in spiritual progress. A directive emerges from our faith experience and is a pointer on the journey to deeper faith in God. Consequently, "a person must be extremely careful always to let go this knowledge, and desire to journey to God by unknowing."

---

[6]See *Contemplation*, pp. 53-84.

We must eventually let go all specific directives in order to follow to the end God's own spiritual direction within us.

In his sketch of the Ascent of Mount Carmel, St. John of the Cross depicts a mountain with three paths leading upward. The two winding paths on either side come to a dead end. Needless to say, these are the ways of the attached person. The third path — the straight and narrow — goes up the center. This is the way of *nada, nada, nada*. But interestingly enough it does not go all the way to the top. About half way up it peters out. And in that space where we would assume it should have continued, John indicates this stark truth: Hereon out there is no way because there is no law. Beyond a certain point even the way of *nada* gives way to pure faith in God himself. This is the zenith of the freedom of the children of God (*Rm* 8:21).

So, too, beyond a certain point God's spiritual direction no longer comprises specific direction. This is divine wisdom at its wisest (1 *Co* 1:25).

*Chapter 8*

# The Emergence of the Directee's Spiritual Direction

In ordinary parlance, we say that the sun rises and that the sun sets. Yet, we know that this manner of speech is not scientifically correct. We say also that a spiritual director gives direction and that the directee receives it from him/her. Yet, we know that this is not theologically accurate. Both the director and the directee discern God's direction already present and operative within the directee. The question which we address in this chapter is, therefore, the following: How does the already existing spiritual direction emerge into the directee's consciousness?

Listening to God, directees become conscious of their already existing direction in two ways: (1) immediately from God, or (2) mediately through a director (or through some other means like a book, homily, etc.).

(1) Without any assistance from a director, directees can discover for themselves their own particular direction. They may then authenticate this discovery with a director.

This direction may have been seen prior to meeting with the director. Frequently too, in the act of verbalizing to the director their struggle and confusion directees perceive on their own the appropriate direction. In these instances, through the director, the Spirit gives them positive confirmation of their personal discernment or the challenge necessary to unmask their illusion.

(2) On the other hand, the Spirit may reveal first to the director the proper direction for a directee through the discernment process itself.

In such instances, God uses the director's words and silence to awaken directees to a consciousness of what is already operative within them. This may come about as a result of specific questions, suggestions or observations. Thus, the director interprets and explicates what s/he sees happening in the directees.

For their part, directees must discern carefully the director's advice. Is the direction compatible with their inner thrust? Does it resonate? Are they at home with this guidance? Assuming that the advice is compatible, they may acknowledge readily the authenticity of the directive. Yet they may need to have many illusions dispelled before they are capable of accepting peacefully all the implications of this discovery.

## A. Preconditions

There are at least four preconditions necessary in directees so that the emergence of their spiritual direction can take place:

### (1) SOLITARY PRAYER

By solitary prayer, we refer to the example of Jesus who continually went off to some solitary place in order to be alone with his Father (*Lk* 5:16). This prayer may be discursive or contemplative, depending on how the Spirit leads. But what is of paramount importance is the quality of one's listening: that is, of one's loving attentiveness to God.

This loving encounter with God opens directees both to the truth of God and to the truth of themselves. It awakens in them not only a deeper experience of the love of God, but also a greater realization of their own innate sinfulness and infidelity, their alienation from God and others, their need for reconciliation and healing.

In facing their inner poverty, directees have to be willing to undergo being stripped by God of their illusions and attachments, their defenses and egocentricity. Unless directees are willing to abandon themselves to God and submit in silence and solitude of the heart to his transforming and purifying love, it is useless for them to seek help from a spiritual director. The Spirit empowers directees to discern only if they listen first to God: "Give your servant a listening heart so as to be able to discern" (1 *Kg* 3:9).

## (2) DESIRE FOR TRUTH

An honest desire for truth facilitates greatly the emergence of spiritual direction.

Yet, while truth intensifies freedom and interior peace (*Jn* 8:32), it is often bitter medicine to swallow. Truth necessarily purges all that is untruthful. It uproots and detaches, corrects and reproves, often thrusting one in directions one would rather not follow. It requires that directees let go even their very selves and turn more radically to God with their whole being.

Do our directees show honest receptivity and openness? Are they obstinate, stubborn, closed-minded? Are they willing to change? Are they seeking confirmation of their illusions? Are they looking for praise and esteem for their supposedly spiritual experiences?

It is easy to say that one seeks truth, but just how efficacious that desire actually is becomes evident in one's response to challenge, questioning or confrontation. Some directees want truth provided that the personal cost is not too high. They are unwilling to commit themselves to seek truth in a way that radically transforms their being and revolutionizes their lives. These directees put limits on truth. They are disposed to go only so far. They may even perceive partial truth, but their constant compromise, complacency and rationalization impede the emergence of the whole truth.

Strictly speaking, truth does not admit of degrees. A person seeks either the whole truth or none at all. A half-truth is not *the* truth. Jesus is the truth (*Jn* 14:6; 18:38). Unless directees seek truth in all its fullness, spiritual direction proves fruitless.

### (3) OPENNESS TO OUTCOME

The sole purpose of discernment is to discover God's will and the manner in which a person can best collaborate with it. Therefore, directees need openness to *whatever* direction the Spirit reveals. They have to be ready to follow in dark faith, wherever the Spirit leads.

This intensity of abandonment to God in faith presupposes that directees possess a certain objectivity in discernment. They must be able to transcend their own personal preferences. Prayerful consideration of every aspect of the matter in question, while remaining open to every possible solution or outcome, is a necessary requirement for the emergence of spiritual direction.

Directees cannot select beforehand only certain directions which they would be willing to pursue. Nor can they eliminate any possible avenues until each has been adequately discerned. Directees have to be willing to go any way that the Spirit indicates, whether or not this way accords with their personal likes.

The principal obstacle to openness with respect to the outcome of a discernment process is usually a person's fixation on some particular way or result. Some directees can so blindly latch onto their own desire that they render themselves incapable of listening to God, much less anyone else.

### (4) WILLINGNESS TO WAIT WITH PATIENCE

Directees have to wait patiently upon God who in his time and in his way will surely reveal the necessary direction (*Rm*

8:25). Our return to the Father is characterized by a straining forward in eager expectation (*Ph* 3:13). Patience enables directees, while they are moving forward, to live fully in the present, to listen to God as he speaks in the here and now. Even though they may not comprehend how, the Spirit is nonetheless already guiding them to a clearer perception of the way forward.

## B. Emergence

God's spiritual direction is not always immediately apparent to either the directee or the director. Especially when the discernment centers around vocation in life and the deeper movements of prayer, the search can be quite prolonged and intricate. Although God's direction already exists within directees, it must be given birth. It must be born into consciousness by the Spirit with much travail and patience (*Rm* 8:18-25).

In such instances, to discern their spiritual direction directees pass through the normal process of divergence and convergence to reach emergence.

Directees explore first many divergent possibilities and alternatives in their lived experience. In searching through various options, they eliminate gradually certain ones which they discern to be incompatible with their inner self. This phase necessarily yields many blind alleys and dead ends. To discover what their spiritual direction is, directees usually have to discover first what their spiritual direction is *not*. It is normal that they make many mistakes and commit their share of faults. No one can learn by experience and escape unscathed.

The phase of divergence — spiritual adolescence, as it were — does not continue indefinitely. Gradually, directees begin to converge upon a few possibilities with which they intuitively experience affinity. If they pursue these converging directions long enough and deeply enough, their spiritual direction will emerge finally into consciousness. Directees then reach spiritual adulthood. This pattern leads paradoxically to full-blown spiritual childhood (*Mt* 18:2-4). "At first, wisdom may take us through winding ways, bringing fear and faintness upon us, plaguing us with her discipline until she can trust us. Wisdom tests with her ordeals. But in the end she will lead us back to the straight road and reveal her secrets to us" (*Si* 4:17-18). .

As spiritual directors, we must remember that directees seek guidance at a particular point in this process of divergence, convergence and emergence. This is true both in terms of their salvation history as a whole as well as of the specific issue that they may be currently seeking to discern. Occasionally we go through the entire process with them. More often, however, we listen with them for only a limited time. They move on eventually to complete the process elsewhere.

We should ascertain in a general way where directees are situated in this process. This will enable us to facilitate their movement towards the emergence of the appropriate spiritual direction. Moreover, we can also help them see their searching, struggle and disappointments in proper perspective. Directees must realize that they are not necessarily drifting aimlessly. The perplexities of their experience could be integral to true searching.

## C. Follow-up Discernment

The director frequently encounters resistance in directees after a spiritual direction has emerged. The source of this resistance can be either God or the directees themselves.

On the one hand, their resistance to a particular directive may arise from the Spirit. In this case, the resistance indicates that a certain direction is not in fact from God. Thus, directees would be struggling with God against a way that is not from him. This positive resistance persists in them even when they try to deny it or to force themselves to move in an inappropriate direction. For instance, if God has not gifted a certain priest with a celibate vocation, that priest cannot continue indefinitely living and growing celibately. He cannot resist his inner resistance for very long (*Jr* 20:9).

On the other hand, resistance may indicate that directees are struggling against God, against the specific way towards which the Spirit is drawing them. Sometimes their initial reaction to the emergence of a certain direction is rebellion and withdrawal. It may take a while before directees are willing to let themselves be led along God's way (*Jr* 1:6; 20:7-9).

Even when sincere acceptance of one's spiritual direction exists in one's innermost being, resistance may persist simultaneously on other levels: especially emotional and psychological. Jesus himself experienced this paradox during his passion. His soul was troubled unto death (*Jn* 12:27). Yet he remained wholly abandoned to his Father. His emotions and psyche were in a state of such anxiety that he sweat blood, praying: "Father, if you are willing, take this cup away from me. Nonetheless, not my will, but yours be done" (*Lk* 22:42).

Thus, assuming a particular direction or directive is from God, the resistance to it may derive from a threefold poverty: (1) from the poverty of the directee resisting the truth of the direction; (2) from the poverty of the director who intermingles parts of him/herself with a directive which is still basically from God; and (3) from the poverty of the direction itself. It may be too mysterious to be assimilated all at once.

What signs indicate to directees that a particular direction is in fact from God? They are basically seven:

## (1) CONSISTENT RECURRENCE

Having given themselves sufficient time in solitary prayer and in discernment with their guides, directees experience a consistent drawing towards a certain direction. While sincerely examining other possibilities, they find themselves returning constantly to a particular one.

No one can be absolutely sure that a given directive is from God. Proofs of an empirical nature are superfluous and contrary to growth in faith. All that directees need is the recognition that the spiritual influences which they are undergoing favor a certain direction. They then follow it. The further they go, the more they experience a mysterious inability not to pursue it. This inability to do otherwise is a compelling sign of authenticity.

## (2) CONTINUITY AND DISCONTINUITY

The direction which emerges for directees is both in prolongation of and in rupture with their spiritual journey thus far.

Their inner direction is in continuity with their past. They are the same persons now as before. In some mysterious way, their spiritual genesis has always had an innate thrust towards the direction which is presently emerging. Yet there is necessarily also some discontinuity. For in moving forward they leave something behind.[1]

## (3) CONFIRMATION BY OTHERS

After careful discernment, agreement among the directee, his/her legitimate authority (e.g., superior or community in the case of a religious; spouse or family in the case of married persons) and his/her director is a strong indication that a given direction is really from God. Disagreement among the parties involved indicates usually that instead of embarking immediately upon the direction in question, the directee should continue discernment.

God always bestows his graces in the raw. The concrete form which he intends them to take is rarely, if ever, as we initially envisage it.

## (4) PEACE

In following their particular direction, directees experience "the peace which the world cannot give" (*Jn* 14:27).

[1] See *Receptivity*, pp. 114-120.

This peace accompanies an undeniable conviction that to be true to God and to themselves they cannot do other than proceed voluntarily in the direction indicated. Since it is so deep, this peace may coexist with considerable anxiety, hesitancy, uncertainty and fear of the unknown.

## (5) THE FRUITS OF THE SPIRIT

When self-indulgence is at work the results are obvious: sexual irresponsibility, superstition, resentments, wrangling, strife, rivalries, dissension, envy, drunkenness, excesses of all kinds. "But the fruit of the Spirit is very different: love, joy, peace, patience, kindness, goodness, fidelity, gentleness, and self-discipline" (*Ga* 5:19-23). "By their fruits you will know them" (*Mt* 7:16).

## (6) CONTINUED QUESTIONING

Directees do not proudly claim absolute certainty that a particular directive or direction is from God. Nor do they rationalize away every reservation that is expressed by others with respect to the direction in question. Rather, an attitude of humble faith prevails.

They acknowledge that, as well as they can discern, God seems to be indicating a given direction. They admit readily the possibility of error. They remain open to receive further direction from the Spirit, even direction which goes contrary to what stands at present. Only sincere persons are aware of the possibility of their own insincerity. Only honest persons recognize how easily they can be deluded by their own ways, preferences and desires.

## (7) PERSEVERANCE IN LIVING ONE'S SPIRITUAL DIRECTION

The lived experience is an irrefutable criterion. Ultimately, the authenticity of any direction is proven by living it out.

Perseverance in this context cannot come from will power alone. It is a God-given ability enabling directees to fulfill what he sends them forth to accomplish. Perseverance is then a sign of God's loving presence within them. It is a sign that he is upholding and sustaining them by his power and strength, a sign that the direction which they are following is indeed from him.

The Spirit imparts spiritual direction in order to thrust directees ever deeper into the mystery of Christ. Not only do they perceive their direction by faith, but also they act upon it in faith.

True direction, while filled with the peace of Christ, in no way envelops directees in clarity, security and precision. In fact, the directive which emerges may itself be quite dark and nebulous. Both the directee and the director may remain perplexed for some time about its full meaning and ultimate implications.

Having embarked upon a certain direction, directees arrive eventually at a point where they let go both the director and the directive in order to follow wherever the direction leads. They take that leap into greater mystery, allowing God to lead them forward along a way they do not know. Yet, no sooner do these directees continue their journey to God by unknowing than once again they experience the need to search for further spiritual direction. Thus, the process repeats itself with the emergence of each new directive containing the invitation to deeper life in faith and greater convergence in Christ. "Do you believe because you have seen me? Blessed are those who do not see and yet believe" (*Jn* 20:29).

Ultimately, there comes a threshold where directees not only let go their director and his/her directives, but also they let go even the direction itself. They abandon that way in order to surrender completely to him who is *the* Way: the person of Jesus Christ (*Jn* 14:6). "On this road" to transforming union in love "to lose one's way is to enter upon the way. In other words, to pass on to the goal and to leave one's own way is to enter upon that which has no way at all: God.

For the soul who arrives at this state" of total abandonment "no longer has any ways of its own ... although it does have within itself all ways, like one who possesses nothing (*nada*), yet possesses all (*todo*)."[2]

---

[2] *Ascent*, II, 4, 5.

*Chapter 9*

# Difficulties for the Director in Listening

Certain tendencies which may exist within the director impede the listening process. Those most frequently encountered are: selectivity in listening, counter-transference, inadequate balance between firmness and gentleness, and hesitancy to risk.

## A. Selectivity

The great mass of information which inundates our consciousness far exceeds our capacity for assimilation. Our ability to absorb sensory input is sorely limited. Out of everything that comes at us we quite naturally select what we consider to be in accord with our personal interests, needs and preferences.

Take the example of several people standing on a mountain top. They relish the panoramic view of the surrounding countryside. Without adverting to the fact, only certain details of the whole attract the attention of each individual. Numerous other details escape notice. Should one later describe to another the scene they had both observed, each might be amazed at the other's different impressions.

Similarly, in the process of education we tend to select those areas which best suit our talents, needs and personal interests. These may be in music, literature, science, history, sports, etc. Our selectivity affects even our choice of career and our choice of friends.

Such selectivity has a positive dimension. Respecting the limitations of self, time and energy, wise selectivity affords us the opportunity to choose those things which most positively foster our development. Selectivity in this sense also enables us to be more quality-oriented. Rather than skim a mass of material, for example, we study more comprehensively a single topic or question.

No matter how positive an influence selectivity is in our lives, it does in fact limit us. When we opt for a particular direction, this act excludes of necessity other possibilities.

Selectivity becomes manifestly negative when choices are made on the basis of prejudice. Prejudice by definition is irrational. By prejudice, we become fixated on something in such a way that we cannot perceive reality. Prejudice colors our whole vision of life, because it inevitably leads us to select only that which reinforces our bias.

A positive kind of selectivity transpires in spiritual direction. This occurs when the Spirit gives the director the wisdom to see which aspects of the directee's experience need more immediate consideration.

Suppose that a directee expresses concern about the authenticity of his/her prayer, love for God and fidelity to him. Out of the mass of perceptions received, the director discerns that the difficulty does not lie specifically with the directee's prayer, love of God or fidelity. Rather the crux of the problem is preoccupation with self. The directee insists on knowing precisely what is happening in prayer. The directee cannot rest until s/he feels love for God, or feels faithful. In effect, such a person is not living by faith, and does not really trust God or his mysterious ways. The director then selects this lack of faith and trust for more discussion.

However, selectivity in any sense other than the ability to recognize those areas which need discernment constitutes a potential obstacle in listening to God.

Let us consider certain instances in which selectivity affects negatively the listening process:

(1) Excessive concentration on one area of difficulty in the directee's life can lead directors to exclude other important areas. This mistaken selectivity occurs, for example, when we overemphasize the significance of a past event or when we neglect the positive means now available for the directee to continue forward.

(2) Especially if we are inexperienced directors, we may exaggerate the importance of some difficulty which is in fact of only minor significance for the directee. This can happen when we are uncomfortable with having no particular direction to give. Feeling that we should be saying or doing something, we select some point and try to make an issue of it.

(3) Some directors on occasion encourage a directee to overlook a difficulty which is similar to one which they are repressing or denying in their own life. Encouraging the directee to explore his/her difficulty would require that they themselves face their own lack of response to God. For example, the director who does not personally experience the positive value of the cross easily reinforces a directee's negative attitude towards suffering or encourages him/her to avoid asceticism or self-discipline.

(4) Selectivity can proceed from unrealistic expectations on our part with regard to the directee. In listening, we then focus only on those signs which tend to confirm the righteousness of our expectations. Such expectations can lead us to form a preconceived image or idea of the directee, thereby disregarding the uniqueness of the individual. So dominant may these expectations be that we block out anything to the contrary. For example, we imagine that the directee is called to the religious life. Selectivity in listening will lead us to pick up only what tends to affirm this illusion. It will blind us to the presence of positive signs of a call elsewhere.

(5) Sometimes selectivity leads us to reject those dimensions of the directee's self-disclosure which are incompatible with our personal prejudices.

Take the example of a mother who experiences a call to more solitary prayer than the circumstances of her life easily permit. If an incompetent director believes that quiet prayer is in itself a waste, that person belittles the whole idea. Selectivity arising from this prejudice leads this director to disregard a priori any possibility of authenticity in the mother's desire for more solitude.

Again, suppose we have a prejudice against all structured forms of religious life. This bias leads us to assume that a directee could not possibly be called to a given congregation or order. We then unconsciously select only those indications which suggest that the directee does not have a religious vocation.

Sometimes directors cannot see beyond weaknesses associated with certain personality types. Some directors are repelled by shy, silent types, while others look with disdain upon dependent, disturbed types. The lack of acceptance of a particular directee in his/her weakness arises frequently from our denial or repression of the same or a similar weakness in ourselves.

(6) The assumption that we know the directee through and through also can give rise to selectivity in listening. In this instance, we give advice based on illusory preconceptions of the directee.

Any presumption of thorough knowledge of a directee's interior life results in underestimation or overestimation of that person. The former restricts the directee's freedom and capacity to grow, while the latter produces anxiety in the directee at being unable to measure up to our unrealistic expectations.

No matter how well we know a directee, we cannot assume that this knowledge is complete. There are always greater depths to be fathomed. Furthermore, by virtue of the transforming and consuming activity of God within him/her the directee is always in the process of self-transcendence.

Thus, selectivity in listening leads directors to blow out of proportion a real though minor problem or to imagine great difficulty where little or none exists. It leads us to focus upon only what accords with our expectations, to interpret signs in accordance with our prejudices, to distort reality in order to maintain a false conception of a directee. In being negatively selective, we close ourselves off from whatever does not accord with our egocentrism.

Consequently, spiritual direction becomes a charade with no grounding in reality or in life. The real mystery of God within the directee eludes us. We urge the directee to pursue directions which are contrary to his/her inner thrust. The inevitable result of these tendencies is spiritual deformation and misdirection.

## B. *Counter-transference*

Transference is a phenomenon which takes place in many counseling and psychotherapeutic situations. It occurs in the counselee inasmuch as s/he relates to the counselor as if the counselor were someone else. The counselee displaces feelings, expectations, etc. which originate in other relationships. Transference can occur also in a directee with regard to his/her spiritual director. At the outset of spiritual direction, we may sometimes tolerate transference as a possible disposing factor for the directee. The directee may have to work through the immaturities which transference implies before being able to relate to us in a more mature manner. This tolerance cannot continue indefinitely however, because if it does, it will surely impede the directee's ability to listen.

Counter-transference is transference in reverse. It refers to unrealistic or inappropriate behavior on the part of the director with respect to the directee. It is never helpful in spiritual direction, since it necessarily runs counter to the listening process.

Counter-transference is manifested when the director relates to a directee as if s/he were some other person. We displace onto the directee emotions, presumptions and correlations which originate in other relationships. In short, we put another face on the directee and proceed to act accordingly.

For instance: The directee may remind us of our mother or father so much so that we relate to the directee in some situations as if s/he really were. The directee may remind us of an intimate friend so much so that we displace onto the directee some of the attraction or passionate feelings proper to that other relationship. We could also see the directee as resembling ourselves. We may tend in this instance to identify the personality, life experience and future direction of the directee too much with our own.

Counter-transference can comprise positive or negative feelings or attitudes. If our relationship with our mother is loving and affectionate, we may displace these positive feelings onto the directee who resembles her. On the other hand, if we are hostile and resentful towards our mother, we may transfer these same negative feelings to the directee who reminds us of her.

Counter-transference occurs also when our personal needs are interjected into the relationship with the directee. In this case we use the directee for personal gratification. We may, for example, have a strong need to care for others. While in itself this need can be healthy — indeed integral to a vibrant Christian life — it can also become misdirected. Inordinate caring is evident when our feelings of sympathy for the directee control our judgment. This situation leads us to take a course of action or give advice which results not from listening to the Spirit but from our emotional reactions.

Let us assume, for example, that a person is at a radical turning point in his/her life: perhaps in the process of seeking a divorce or of requesting a dispensation from religious vows. If we are inordinately sympathetic, we begin making and executing decisions for the directee. We may go well out of our way to secure employment for the directee, or actually become the manager of his/her finances and personal property. We may begin socializing unnecessarily with the directee. All of this transpires under the guise of being supportive and of keeping the directee from making a mistake.

On the other hand, we may be inordinately seeking to gratify our need to be loved, especially if intimate relationships are lacking in our personal life. Signs of this include: frequently phantasizing about the directee as lover or intimate friend, creating opportunities in spiritual direction to elicit praise or approval from him/her, seeking undue physical signs of affection from the directee, always trying to please him/her, delving unnecessarily into the directee's psychosexual development.

A relationship that brings together a protective director and a dependent directee also contains traces of countertransference. The tendency to protect and to shelter the directee is often closely related to a need within the director to dominate. A directee's tendency to be dependent can arise from a desire to appear weaker and more helpless than s/he really is. This kind of dependency has nothing to do with poverty of spirit. Rather it is a form of seductiveness which seeks to control the other. The dependent person wants someone to cling to, to lean upon. Therefore, s/he manipulates the other into this posture. Of course, the other may be only too happy to oblige. One inordinate need thus complements the other. While the protective director seeks a dependent directee, the dependent directee relishes a protective director. In the final analysis, they both fall into the pit (*Mt* 15:14).

A dependent directee craves the attention which a protective director lavishes upon him/her. Frequently, when an expression of protectiveness is not forthcoming, this directee uses subtle and sometimes obvious means to draw it forth. When the director withholds his/her usual protection, the dependent directee feels rejected, upset, confused and may throw a tantrum.

In the genesis of a spiritual director-directee relationship, some signs of protection and dependency fall at times within normal limits. None of us is perfect (*Ph* 3:12, 15). However, if the respective protection and dependency are too deep-seated, the only remedy may be to sever the relationship.

Disrespect, dislike or outright hostility toward a directee because s/he does not conform to the director's expectations may also indicate a kind of counter-transference. In this case, the director reacts more to the behavior of the directee than to the directee as person.

How are we as directors to deal constructively with the ever present potential for counter-transference?

We should not deny or repress these feelings if and when they occur. To do so would allow them to control and dominate us. We listen to our feelings, identify as clearly as possible the nature of the counter-transference and accept what is happening. By understanding our feelings, the freedom will come to let go our projections and to see directees as they really are. At times seeking out spiritual direction for ourselves or consultation with another competent and experienced director can also help resolve counter-transference.

The common factor in all counter-transference is the inability of the director to see directees as they truly are. If not corrected, counter-transference necessarily obstructs spiritual direction from emerging. We cannot listen to God in directees until we first accept them as they are before him.

## C. Inadequate Balance between Firmness and Gentleness

Firmness without gentleness on the part of the director results in gruffness, harshness and severity. The brash director, contrary to his/her call to remain servant, will "break the crushed reed; quench the wavering flame" (*Is* 42:3). Such behavior can have a devastating effect on the directee in that it tends towards depersonalization.

The harsh director becomes the accusing voice that sees no good in directees. S/he tears down self-confidence and gradually destroys the positive attitude of directees towards themselves. This director can lower self-esteem in directees, leaving them with a sense of worthlessness and rejection.

Paradoxically, a directee who has an inordinate need for attention may return repeatedly to a harsh, severe director. A person can be so starved for affection that this form of attention is better than none at all. In fact, when the director shows no particular emotion, such a person may even attempt to get attention by provoking the director. This smacks of masochism.

Quite often, however, the perception of harshness or severity in a director is in reality an illusion on the part of directees. This illusion arises usually from unresolved past experiences of personal rejection. It may be indicative also of a bent towards isolation. Directees may be seeking to remain in their own comfortable, secure world without disturbance and without challenge. Directees who are falling more and more into self-analysis, introspection and self-pity, for instance, require a firm hand to guide them out of their egocentrism. Yet, they complain to the director: You are being too hard on me. You are hurting me. These directees are really saying: Leave me alone. Don't disturb my tidy little nest. Let me wallow in myself.

As directors, we must gently but with uncompromising firmness address the true needs of the directee. We have to pursue this course even when directees complain unjustifiably of being harshly treated.

While firmness without gentleness is destructive of the listening process, gentleness without firmness can be equally harmful. Lack of firmness leads us to placate the directee. This behavior acquiesces to a directee's whims and fancies.

To placate is almost always a misguided expression of love or sympathy. It may represent an attempt to gain personal acceptance or to spare directees the pain necessary for their growth.

Placating obstructs listening. Not only does it allow directees to continue unchecked in their self-indulgence and laxity, but also it gives the impression of confirming directees in these immaturities. These directees are left unchallenged, and are encouraged on their course towards ever greater interior dissipation. This can result only in estrangement from self, from others and from God.

Nonetheless, there are occasions when the Spirit moves us to take a more lenient than usual approach with a certain directee. Suppose, for example, a directee tends to be excessively demanding of him/herself, be it out of scrupulosity, self-effacement, whatever. Should we respond to a real failure on the part of this person by being too demanding, this could easily reinforce his/her basic lack of self-acceptance, and accomplish nothing of spiritual benefit for the perplexed directee.

St. Therese of the Child Jesus, as spiritual director, summarizes well many of these points: "In ministering to others, I have learned much. I have seen above all that all souls have almost the same struggles, but that these souls are so very different from each other.... It is impossible to act with all in the same manner. With certain souls, I feel that I must be little, never fearing to humble myself by confessing my own struggles and defeats.... With others, however, I have seen that to do any good for them I must be quite firm and never back down from what I say."[1]

We must thus discern in each instance which approach most effectively assists directees in discovering their spiritual direction.

## D. Hesitancy to Take Risks

Reluctance to risk can originate from a variety of sources: a desire for certitude and control, a lack of confidence, fear of making a mistake, pride, timidity, etc. The refusal to take risk stifles the Spirit. While it prevents certain pitfalls, it also removes the possibility of maximum spiritual growth.

The basis of spiritual direction is complete abandonment to God in openness and receptivity. This act by its very nature necessitates the willingness to take risk, for God's ways are not our ways (*Is* 55:8-9).

Risk is not necessarily opposed to prudence. In fact, in the context of spiritual direction the willingness to take risk

[1] *Therese*, pp. 239-240.

actually assists us in acting according to what we discern to be the will of God for the directee. To take a prudent risk is to make an act of faith. *Tutius non est verius*: What is safer is not necessarily truer. What really paralyzes life in the Spirit is lack of faith in God and refusal to risk. The pusillanimous person has neither faith in God nor in self, only in the status quo.[2]

[2]See *Receptivity*, pp. 112-114.

*Chapter 10*

# Difficulties for the Directee in Listening

Certain problems within the directee also tend to obstruct the emergence of spiritual direction. The principal ones are: unrealistic expectations, pride, legalism, desire to control the director, undue tension between the sacrament of reconciliation and spiritual direction, transference and personality disorders.

## A. Unrealistic Expectations

Some people approach spiritual direction quite unrealistically. They expect and demand immediate results. They think of spiritual direction as a problem-solving device. They expect the director to provide a ready answer to every difficulty. When an answer is not immediately forthcoming, they become increasingly frustrated, impatient and demanding. This type of person is frequently one who is insecure, who wants to be told what to do, who shirks personal responsibility, who is not at peace with the mysterious ebbs and flows of life.

The myth of immediacy is also evident in persons who expect rapid, observable progress. These persons try too hard. They take God's business into their own hands. They seek perfection by their own initiative and effort rather than by receptivity to and cooperation with God's initiative. This attitude leads to further frustration and confusion.

Learning to wait on God with patient hope is often a hard lesson in life, but a salvific one. God alone is our Savior. And fortunately for us, he will not let us forget it. Spiritualization is a gradual process. We must learn to accept our weaknesses and limitations peacefully (2 *Co* 12:9). We have to continue patiently straining forward without becoming unduly discouraged (*Ph* 3:13).

As directors we greatly assist our directees dispel their myth of immediacy by patiently waiting for God to effect change in them. We accomplish nothing by demanding change before its time. Like the prodigal father, we must give directees enough freedom, space and trust to make their own mistakes. Yet, we have to remain always ready to receive them back with open arms once conversion has occurred (*Lk* 15:11-20).

Some directees are too product-oriented. They entertain the false expectation that something perceptible must happen during every meeting with their director. Such persons consider a waste of time and energy any session in which no apparent direction emerges. If nothing is forthcoming on several consecutive occasions, they begin to brood that their director no longer cares for or understands them. They complain that the director just sits there saying nothing. Full of self-pity, these persons accuse their director of no longer being effective, and consider changing directors or terminating spiritual direction altogether.

The directee and the director must patiently trust in God and be content to listen despite the absence of specific directives. The absence of particular directives can in fact be God's way of directing. Although the directee may feel a need for something tangible, God may want him/her to continue to journey in dark faith without knowing the way.

Even when there is an authentic need for spiritual guidance, the Spirit may not immediately grant enlightenment. Patient and often prolonged searching is usually necessary before the directee is sufficiently disposed to receive God's direction.

Some directees expect the director to agree with everything they say. They seek unquestioning affirmation rather than spiritual direction. Should we confront them, ask challenging questions or make suggestions that differ from their current ideas or practices, they become indignant and defensive: How dare you tell me what to do! What right have you to intrude on my privacy?

Merton observes: Some souls "are not pleased with the available director because he does not flatter their self-esteem or cater to their illusions about themselves. In other words, they want a director who will confirm their hope of finding pleasure in themselves and in their virtues, rather than one who will strip them of their self-love and show them how to get free from preoccupation with themselves and their own petty concerns, to give themselves to God and to the Church."[1]

## B. Pride

Pride is operative when directees cling obstinately or arrogantly to a god of their own making, whether this be their opinions, attitudes, self-image or their rugged individualism.

Spiritual pride is particularly obstructive of the listening process. The overall tone and manner with which directees reveal their life experiences reveal the presence or absence of humility. Pride touches virtually everyone to some degree. St. John of the Cross notes: "Some have more, others less, while still others have only the first movements or little

[1]*S. Direction*, p. 22.

more. There is scarcely anyone who is not troubled by some snare of pride."[2]

Spiritual pride generates a false sense of being already perfect, of having already arrived. This in turn leads to interior mediocrity and complacency.

Pride is evident in persons who act as if they themselves were the source of their own graces and blessings. Instead of humbly giving glory to God (*Lk* 1:46-49), they use these spiritual gifts for self-glorification.

Proud persons are full of their own imagined importance. Using the gifts of God for their self-centered ends, they seek to display *their* wisdom, *their* holiness, *their* virtues, etc. "They develop a vain liking for speaking of spiritual things in the presence of others, and sometimes even for teaching these things rather than for being taught."

Their piosity is often apparent in their body language: "Such persons contrive to give exterior manifestations of their assumed holiness in movements, sighs and other ceremonies. At times they even swoon as if in ecstacy. Of course, all this happens in public rather than in private ... for they are quite pleased, indeed eager, that others notice these things."

In order to gain attention and praise, spiritually proud persons force certain practices upon themselves. Some want to appear humble by keeping their heads bowed and eyes downcast. Others try to give the impression of ecstasy by maintaining a smirky facial expression. Some of these latter flutter their eyelids or roll their eyeballs, while others keep their eyes tightly closed. Spiritual pride may also be at the source of excessive religious garb, of forced efforts to speak pious things, of ostentatious prostrations and bows.

Spiritually proud persons are usually very judgmental, critical and condescending towards others. "In their heart, they condemn others when they do not appear to have the kind of devotion that they would like them to have. Some-

---

[2] *Night*, I, 2, 1-8. The same reference applies to all quotations unless otherwise identified in this section.

times they express their criticism in words. Thus, they act like the pharisee who despised the publican while boasting and praising God for the good works he himself had performed (*Lk* 18:11-12)."

This pride can be so deep-seated that it engenders envy to the point of vengeance. These people "desire that no one but themselves appear good. Thus by word and deed they condemn and slander others whenever the opportunity arises, seeing the speck in their brother's eye but failing to consider the plank in their own (*Mt* 7:3). They strain the other's gnat and themselves swallow the camel (*Mt* 23:24)."

Directees with a know-it-all attitude are often enmeshed in spiritual pride. Such persons respond to practically everything the director says with arrogant self-assurance. "When someone tries to instruct them, they themselves take the words out of the other's mouth as if they already knew it all." As long as this attitude persists, it is virtually impossible to listen to the Spirit.

Spiritually proud people "ordinarily want to discern their spirit only with someone whom they think will praise them and be impressed by what they do.... They flee those who would change them. Sometimes they even harbor ill will against such spiritual directors."

When corrected or given advice contrary to their preferences, these proud directees claim that they are misunderstood or that the director is unspiritual because s/he does not approve of their way.

As directors we need to be attentive to whether there exists within our directees a balance between the awareness of their blessings and the realization of their poverty. Persons who constantly sing their own praises without acknowledgement of their poverty are living a life steeped in illusion. If faults are pointed out to them, they try to deny these faults or excuse themselves rather than accept personal responsibility. At times, they admit some responsibility, but downplay the seriousness of the fault itself.

The opposite is equally harmful: those who exaggerate their poverty and can see nothing good in themselves. These persons maintain a low self-esteem. They suffer from a lack of affirmation and love. But in their own way, they can also be proudly trying to manipulate indirect praise and pity from their director.

Merton warns: "The director must be on his guard against the unconscious spiritual vanity which makes virtuous souls" — and the not so virtuous — "seek to shine, in a subtle way, in his eyes and capture his approval.... Nothing does so much harm in direction as the acceptance by the director of an unconscious pretense of perfection" — or of poverty —"in place of the real thing."[3]

Another reaction which proud directees display is this: When faced with their weakness, they become unduly distraught, thinking that they should have already become saints. In their discouragement and despair, these directees become anxious and impatient with themselves and with God. They desperately want God to purify them, not for God's sake, however, but for their own comfort. That want to be at peace and undisturbed by their poverty. "They fail to see that should God remove their imperfections and faults most likely they would become even more proud and presumptuous."

Quite the contrary is the response of humble persons. In the experience of their richness, they recognize all as coming from God and as destined to him (*Lk* 1:46-49). In the experience of their poverty, they undergo their limitations and sinfulness with humility, interior tranquility and unconditional trust in God's loving mercy (2 *Co* 12:10). Furthermore, they remain always open to receive God in whatever manner he chooses to come.

Spiritually proud persons tend to speak of their experiences of God too easily, too freely and with too many people. This is particularly the case when they believe that these experiences appear extraordinary. The truly humble, however, proceed quite differently: "Since the wise Spirit of God dwells within these humble souls, he moves them to keep their treasures within, in secret."

---

[3]*S. Direction*, p. 32.

## C. Legalism

A legalistic attitude which accentuates external conformity with and slavish performance of accepted religious
practices greatly obstructs the listening process.

This propensity drives many to preoccupation with fulfilling laws, observing customs and obeying precepts almost as
ends in themselves. Such persons become more concerned
with getting in their prayers than with truly praying. They
assume a quantitative approach to the interior life, and soon
settle down to the complacent routine of familiar practices
which supposedly multiply merits and indulgences.

Legalists become slaves to the law and mistakenly equate
holiness with the degree of success found in fulfilling the
law's dictates. This attitude quite naturally leads directees to
compare themselves to others. It leads them to expend time
and exert energy competing with others or trying to excel
them spiritually.

Legalism in this context can arise from a number of false
underlying attitudes: (a) Some persons assume that prayer
life is to be equated with the exact performance of external
practices, many of which are self-imposed. Perfection is
gauged by how well one measures up to the established
goals. (b) Other people, forgetting that God alone is their
Savior, set out to save themselves by their own logic, initiative and will. (c) Still others believe that they must conform
to certain religious practices because these appear to be
what everyone else is doing.

A legalistic approach to the interior life renders true
spiritual progress very difficult. Directees so inclined delude
themselves into thinking that they know exactly who they
are, who God is, where they are in relation to God and where
they are going. They thus enfold themselves in an illusory
blanket of comfort, clarity and security. These persons
shield themselves from confronting that vast abyss of their
own nothingness wherein God is most deeply encountered.
Instead of searching for their personal identity in Christ,
they become preoccupied with maintaining their dubious
self-made image.

Directees who pursue this course discover sooner or later that they cannot measure up to their imposed standards of perfection. If after such a realization they still cling to their legalism, they are plagued by increasing anxiety, frustration and discouragement. The more effort they exert to fulfill the law, the more unsuccessful they appear to themselves.

At times these directees are so persistent in their way that they have to hit rock bottom before they are willing to let go. There they experience in every fiber of their being that "no one can be made holy before God by observing the law; rather through the law we become conscious of sin" (*Rm* 3:20). In the experience of their poverty, God opens them to his law: "the law of the Spirit of life in Christ Jesus" (*Rm* 8:2), "the law of faith" (*Rm* 3:27), the law of love (*Rm* 13:8-10).

In other words, at some point such persons begin to move from an exteriorized value system to a more interiorized life. Instead of clinging to externals, they begin living the life of God from within and according to that life's unique destiny in Christ. Only then can a person affirm truthfully with Paul: "I am no longer striving for perfection by my own efforts, the perfection that comes from the law. I want only that perfection which comes through faith in Christ Jesus, and which is from God and is based on faith" (*Ph* 3:9).

When confronted with legalistic directees, we must try first to bring them to at least an initial awareness of the basic problem. We have to encourage them to examine the motivations behind their legalistic attitudes. We need to challenge them to rethink their concepts of God, prayer and self so that they can let go all unnecessary clutter and baggage. We can also help them discover which spiritual devotions and exercises are a truly meaningful, spontaneous response to God's initiative within them.

A directee's transition from quantity to quality may be sudden and dramatic (as with St. Paul) or it may be slow and gradual, almost imperceptible (as with St. Peter). In either case it usually takes some time before the interior change of heart becomes fully integrated into the directee's behavior.

Sometimes it is the director rather than the directee who is more legalistically inclined. The directee may possess a vigorous life in the Spirit, but the legalistic director not understanding the ways of the Spirit tries to impose upon the directee all sorts of spiritual exercises and practices. For instance, the directee is drawn in prayer to remain lovingly attentive to the Beloved, without particular words, gestures or trends of thought. A legalistic director will probably insist that the directee is wasting time and should do something more useful like discursive meditation.

"Many spiritual directors do great harm to many souls because they do not understand the ways and properties of the Spirit. They cause these souls to lose the delicate unctions with which the Holy Spirit gradually anoints them and prepares them for himself. These directors instruct them in lower ways which they themselves have used or have read about somewhere. These ways may indeed be useful for beginners, but knowing no more than how to deal with beginners —please God they knew even that much! — these directors do not permit the soul to go beyond these beginnings with their discursive and imaginary ways (even though God desires to lead them on)."[4]

## D. Desire to Control

Some people have to be in control of every situation. Otherwise, they become defensive, if not openly offensive. At the outset of the director-directee relationship, some persons try to control the quest for spiritual direction. Although this defensiveness is understandable and may be tolerated for a while, directees must come to grips with it if they truly desire to listen.

Here are some examples of how a desire to control is expressed: (a) Although the director is genuinely empathetic, compassionate and receptive, a directee for no appar-

[4]*Flame*, 3, 31.

ent reason accuses him/her of a lack of understanding or of failure to be of assistance. This occurs especially when the director is quietly listening to the directee and to God, but the directee becomes frenzied at receiving no specific direction. (b) A directee continually makes sharp, snappy remarks to the director. These may even be tinged with personal attack. (c) If the director appears younger than the directee, the directee may take a condescending approach: I know how young, uneasy and pressured you must feel at having to direct me; an older, more mature and experienced person.

Such behavior is designed, whether consciously or unconsciously, to goad directors into a defensive posture. It tries also to distract them from the real issue at hand: discovering the directee's spiritual direction.

As directors, we cannot afford to react defensively to the directee by attempting to regain control. Only God should be in control. When either the director or the directee seeks to maintain control, a vicious circle is created which leads to the dissipation of the listening process.

We must keep our attentiveness on God, acting and reacting towards the directee from this listening stance. By ignoring the directee's immature behavior or be steering the discussion back to the proper issues we can sometimes call the person to greater maturity. However, if these indirect approaches are unsuccessful, we may have to resort to direct confrontation.

Although the directee's effort to control is aimed primarily at the director, this behavior is often symptomatic of the directee's response to God as well as to other persons. Therefore, it is usually well to explore the influence of this tendency in all aspects of the directee's life.

## E. Undue Tension between the Sacrament of Reconciliation and Spiritual Direction

For some strange reason, certain directees separate what they confess in the sacrament of reconciliation from what

they disclose in spiritual direction. This compartmentaliza-
tion occurs when they see, in a dichotomizing manner, one
person as their confessor and another as their spiritual
director. Such a dichotomy arises usually from a mistaken
theology of both the sacrament and spiritual direction.

In the tradition of the desert fathers and mothers, celebration of the directee's conversion and reconciliation flowed
spontaneously out of the spiritual direction experience. Frequently, such a celebration crowned months and even years
of painstaking discernment, struggle and repentance. In the
practice of the desert fathers and mothers, the celebration of
penitence was part of spiritual direction, not the other way
around.

Thus, while some spiritual guidance is certainly within the
scope of the sacrament of reconciliation, the praxis of this
sacrament since the middle ages does not lend itself well to
the in-depth and sustained discernment which many people
need. The spiritual guidance received in this sacrament may
be "good advice in itself and perfectly in accordance with
moral theology, and yet, it may not get anywhere near the
real root of the concrete, personal problem in the soul of the
penitent."[5]

To withhold deliberately from the director anything pertaining to personal sin, faults or weaknesses inhibits the
listening process inherent to spiritual direction. Confession
of sin is not of itself essential in spiritual direction. But
admission of actual sinfulness is quite necessary since it
pertains to the directee's innermost struggle and transformation (*Rm* 7:14-25). The director's primary concern is not
with the directee's sins in themselves, but rather with these
acts as symptomatic of deeper immaturity and disorder.
Therefore, the directee must reveal his/her sinfulness to the
director so that together they can discern the source of the
difficulty as well as search out constructive means to correct
it.

[5]*S. Direction*, p. 23. See Monika Hellwig, *Sign of Reconciliation and Conversion* (Michael Glazier, 1982) for some contemporary insight on this question.

True, confession of sin is not of itself essential in spiritual direction, but conversion and repentance certainly are. Moreover, it is normal that sincere directees / penitents want to celebrate this *metanoia* with their spiritual directors / confessors.

## F. Transference

As stated in the previous chapter, the word "transference" refers to that tendency of some directees to put another face on their director. Transference occurs when directees displace onto the director feelings and expectations appropriate to other persons in their lives. A form of transference is also present when directees try to use the relationship with a director to gratify personal needs.

The more aloof a director is, the more a directee tends to transfer. Because such a director is not at home with him / herself, neither can the directee be at ease with him / her. On the other hand, the more mature a director is, the less likelihood there is of any significant transference at all. If some does occur in relation to a mature director, it is apt to be thereby rendered ineffective.

Many directors are self-disciplined and reserved in spiritual direction. Provided that it is natural to these persons, this reserve is the optimal disposition in most instances. Yet, a positive reserve of this kind may still elicit transference in some directees. Many people relate more quickly and more easily with more outgoing personalities. They react to a director's reserve by reverting temporarily to a defensive posture. This behavior attempts to assuage the stark seriousness of the reason for coming together in the first place.

Examples of transference abound: (a) A teenager already experiencing difficulties with his dad seeks direction from a priest called "Father." This adolescent is apt to transfer some of his hostile feelings to the priest. (b) A person with an authority problem may displace emotions felt towards an employer, a religious superior, a pastor, a mother to his/her director. (c) A directee may relate to the current director in a way appropriate to a former spiritual director. (d) A woman who has certain pronounced affective needs, but who does not want to commit herself to anyone, is likely to become attracted to a priest director who is both "Father" and celibate. (e) The overly dependent person who needs somebody —anybody — may seek to lean upon the director for everything.

To deal properly with transference, we must be able first to recognize the behavior of the directee for what it is. Transference is *displaced* feelings, reactions or attitudes. Therefore, we should realize that they are not directed at us personally. There is no reason to become hurt or confused at such behavior. To take the effects of transference personally would tend to thwart the purpose of spiritual direction. Consider once again the teenager who directs his conflicts with his dad towards the director called "Father." Should the priest in question take this as a personal affront, he may try to correct the young man's attitude in a manner reminiscent of the adolescent's own father. This would only reinforce the transference and do nothing to help the youth listen.

We must above all be understanding and accepting of the directee. We should help the directee identify and accept the true source of his/her inappropriate behavior. Take for instance the person who lashes out at the director because s/he does not receive precise answers to difficulties. The director must explore with the directee the possibility that his/her demand for clear and precise answers stems from a desire to be told what to do: that is, from a need for dependency.

Unless deep-seated psychological disorders are present, usually the simple identification and acceptance of the transference are enough to free the directee from its effects. With better self-understanding comes the possibility of transcending feelings and surface needs in order to listen to God.

## G. Personality Disorders

The spiritual director is concerned with discerning the transforming influence of God within the *whole* person in *every* aspect of life. We must, therefore, take into account what is transpiring in the emotional and psychological realms of our directees insofar as this pertains to their spiritual development. However, this should be accomplished without entering into a counseling posture as such. Spiritual direction and counseling of any kind (psychological, personal, emotional, etc.) are not the same, even though in many instances both may be quite complementary and necessary for a given individual.

Everyone has some skeletons in the closet. It is normal to have some immaturities at any point along the path of maturation. Cooperation with grace gradually resolves many of these immaturities in the course of spiritual direction. This maturation occurs frequently without either the director or the directee adverting to the change taking place. It is all part of God's purifying and transforming process.

Counseling or even psychotherapy is necessary when directees become so preoccupied with one aspect of their life that they neglect significantly other important aspects: for example, a person bound up by some phobia, a widow enslaved by a bereavement, a workaholic. These blocks prevent the person from advancing in spiritual, emotional, personal and psychological maturity.

The following frequently encountered difficulties usually require professional help beyond the scope of spiritual direction: a history of unresolved personal rejection by others; the fixation of the directee on some phase of the grieving process after separation from a loved one; low self-esteem to the point of impairing meaningful relationships; uncontrollable anger, rage or resentment; excessive daydreaming, fantasizing; hallucinations; inability to cope with interpersonal conflicts; unresolved sexual identity or frigidity; excessive nervousness, shyness or tension.

At times, it becomes clear to us early in the relationship that the directee needs psychological counseling. At other times, the recognition of this need emerges much later.

Occasionally, we encounter serious difficulty in discerning whether certain behavior patterns are in fact within normal limits. We should not act hastily. Time and patience are always on the side of truth. Practically anyone can benefit from psychological testing and counseling, but surely not everyone needs them. We have to be careful not to overestimate what professional assistance can in fact accomplish. It is a help, not a panacea. Nor must we underestimate what grace can do even psychologically in a truly receptive and listening person.

Where there is doubt concerning the necessity of psychological help, we should usually continue guiding the directee without recommending referral. However, if after a reasonable time there is no significant improvement in the area of difficulty, referral is in order. Consultation with a psychologist or a psychiatrist can prove invaluable in discerning the appropriateness of eventual counseling or therapy.

The manner in which we suggest to a directee the necessity of psychological assistance can have a powerful influence on his/her attitude towards therapy or counseling. Ideally, a person should be led to recognize his/her own need in this area. As a last resort we may have to tell the person what is needed. More often than not, a second opinion is advisable. In any case, no one can ever be helped who does not want to help him/herself. So it behooves us to try always to motivate the directee to seek the appropriate assistance for a given need.

As with everything else we should recommend psychological help to a directee as gently, simply and directly as possible, without embarrassment and without beating around the bush. We should explain insofar as possible why this assistance seems appropriate. This has to be done in a way that conveys to the directee love, acceptance, support and encouragement. Thus, we assist the directee in expressing and transcending negative feelings towards our recommendation.

We must never give the impression that we are abandoning or rejecting the directee or that s/he is beyond our help. No directee is ever completely helpless in that sense.

We should, furthermore, make it clear that this referral does not necessarily mean that spiritual direction must cease altogether. Sometimes it is advisable to continue spiritual direction and professional guidance simultaneously. At times a director and a counselor (or therapist) can work together quite effectively with the same person. Our supportive presence to the directee can be a reminder of God's infinite love as s/he undergoes the painful discoveries and upheaval involved in therapy. We can also help the directee see his/her suffering in a positive and salvific light. We can be an invaluable instrument in helping him/her integrate the insights received through counseling into his/her relationship with God.

*Chapter 11*

# Listening to and Loving the Directee

The director's ability to listen to God within the directee is greatly enhanced by a sincere love for the directee. This truth is a direct application of the Hebrew theology of *ahabh* (love) and *hesed* (steadfast love), as well as of the New Testament's usage of *philos* (friendship), and *agape* (love/charity).

The Torah enjoins each Israelite: "Love your neighbor as yourself" (*Lv* 19:18). Jesus reiterated this same invitation to his disciples, expanding it to include every person, even one's enemies (*Mt* 5:43-48; *Mt* 22:39; *Lk* 10:29-37).

Formulated in this manner, the model for love of others is love of self. Love of others is to be proportionate to love of oneself.

Although Jesus reaffirmed the Torah's injunction, he revealed furthermore that true Christian love far transcends love of self, however important that still remains. In his farewell discourse Jesus proclaims: "This is *my* commandment: love one another as I have loved you" (*Jn* 15:12). How does he love us? "As the Father has loved me, so I have loved you" (*Jn* 15:9). Evangelical love is not limited, therefore, to treating others as we would ourselves. No, we must love as universally, as unselfishly and as honestly as the Father loves his Son who in turn loves us all and gave his life for our salvation. Only thus "will all know that you are my disciples" (*Jn* 13:35).

We are called to love each other as Christ himself loves us with the Father's own love. We must love one another with divine love: that is, with the very love with which the Father loves the Son and the Son loves the Father and who together spirate the Spirit of love. This is a staggering responsibility which can never be fully realized this side of the resurrection. In eternal transforming union we shall love all others in God as God himself loves. In this life, God in us loves God in the other person, while we try to remain always open to love the other with that same love.

This quality of love cannot be attained or achieved. It can only be received from God who is himself love (1 *Jn* 4:7-8). This is, therefore, the love that we mean: not only our love for God and for one another, but especially his love for us in which our love is a participation. "Beloved, if God so loves us, we ought also to love one another" with his own love. "We love because he first loved us" (1 *Jn* 4:11, 19).

Love for others has many faces. There is the love between husband and wife, mother and child, father and son, brother and sister. There is the love of friendship, the love for those to whom we minister, the love for colleagues or associates. Whatever the personal expression of love, the same mystery transpires in varying degrees. This mystery is Christ in me loving Christ in you with the same love with which the Father loves him.[1]

The spiritual director-directee relationship is founded on love and deepens with love. Both the director and the directee are drawn together in the Spirit of love to return with Jesus to the Father. Abiding in God, the director allows Christ within him/her to love and to search for

---

[1]See Augustine's *unus Christus amans seipsum* in his commentary on 1 *Jn* 5:13 (*PL*, 35:2055).

Christ within the directee. The director and the directee interact in a way that is truly loving: "If you hold your peace, do so out of love. If you speak out, do so out of love. If you correct, correct in love. If you spare, spare because of love. Let the root of love be within you. From this root only good can spring forth."[2]

The director's love for the directee is significantly expressed by acceptance, patience, truthfulness, gentleness and competency.

## A. Acceptance

"Love forgives all, trusts all, hopes all, endures all" (1 *Co* 13:7).

Acceptance is a continuous, consistent trust in the basic goodness of another. Acceptance flows from faith in a person coupled with sincere compassion for him/her, whether the person is experiencing success or failure, strength or weakness in his/her efforts to respond to grace.

Acceptance means letting the directee be him/herself in all uniqueness. While acceptance bespeaks love of the person as s/he is, its inner dynamics contain also an invitation to the directee to become more. The director's acceptance invites the directee to self-transcendence.

True acceptance implies recognition of and at homeness with the mystery of personhood. It acknowledges that no matter how well we know the other, something in the other always remains mysteriously beyond our grasp. No matter how deeply and intimately we have shared in another's life, there remains an element of the unknown and unknowable in the person loved. This elusive, ineffable quality, this *no-sé-qué*[3] at its deepest is God himself dwelling within the other's inmost being.

---

[2]Augustine, Commentary on *1 Jn* 4:4-12 (*PL*, 35:2033).
[3]"I-don't-know-what," *Canticle*, stanza 7.

Acceptance (or the lack of it) is radiated through the director's manner of being towards the directee. Acceptance becomes especially perceptible in the equanimity with which we receive all the directee's disclosures. Without being surprised or shocked, judgmental or critical, we listen compassionately to the directee's struggle with God.

The quality of our acceptance encourages the directee in turn to trust us. Thus, the directee experiences enough security and freedom to reveal honestly and frankly his/her inner struggle. The experience of being accepted decreases a person's fear of rejection or of disapproval. It lessens anxiety about living up to assumed expectations. In times of conflict or confrontation, the awareness of being accepted enables the directee to see that we are sincerely seeking his/her greater good.

## B. Patience

"Love is patient.... Love tries to endure whatever happens" (1 *Co* 13:4, 7).

Most people look upon patience as a virtue which any of us can and should acquire, if only we put our mind and heart to it. Certainly we choose to be patient and decide to act patiently, but the patience of which Jesus and St. Paul speak is gift. It is received in us, not acquired by willpower alone. Evangelical patience is an essential quality of enduring love. It is integral to loving receptivity, to true listening, to being deeply with another.

Most of us know all too well what impatience is. But few of us reflect seriously on the real significance and vast implications of patience. Patience arises from love and increases as love intensifies. It is only in love and because of love that patience, extended over a long period of time, becomes perseverance and endures all things. As a virtue, patience is related to courage and fortitude. It is a power, a *dynamis*. Yet, it is not a force of aggressivity, but of Christian passivity and true resignation. Paul intimately links patience (*hypomones*,whose basic meaning in Greek is "to remain") with the eager expectancy (*Rm* 8:25) and the straining forward (*Ph* 3:13) of hope in Christ Jesus. "By patient endurance your souls will be saved" (*Lk* 21:19).

Approaching patience from a somewhat behavioral perspective, St. Augustine describes it as "that by which we endure evil with equanimity so that we may not through a lack of equanimity abandon the good through which we attain something better."[4]

Let us examine Augustine's description:

(1) Patience is exercised with regard to "evil." As such, patience is allied with tolerance. In this life, we endure much evil and adversity. There is that which afflicts us from within: illnesses, psychological disorders, moral weaknesses, effects of personal sin, temptations, etc. There is that which befalls us from without: injustices, selfishness of all kinds, the sin of the world and of others. Evil is whatever constitutes our cross here and now. But in the resurrection there is no further need for patience in this sense. In eternity only love remains (1 *Co* 13:8-13).

(2) We bear our cross and that of others "with equanimity." Equanimity means with equal soul, with the same spirit: "The Lord has given and the Lord has taken away. Blessed be the name of the Lord" (*Jb* 1:21). We have to be as content with the weaknesses, hardships and failures which we undergo for the sake of Christ as we are with our strengths, joys and successes. For in a mysterious way when we are weakest, we are strongest (2 *Co* 12:9-10; 13:4). Yet, this contentment with our weaknesses has nothing to do with complacency or mediocrity. Quite the contrary. We endure evil, while continuing to resist it with all our strength. And even when external resistance is no longer possible, we persist in resisting interiorly. The true Christian never gives in to evil. We never resign ourselves to evil. We are resigned only to God who is encountered in faith through evil and beyond it. Our final human act which

---

[4] *Patience* (*PL*, 40:611-626).

epitomizes our whole life must be towards Life, not towards death.[5]

Patience introduces and maintains the element of equanimity in this process.

(3) Why do we bear our cross patiently? Why do we persevere through the dark night of our soul? "So that we may not abandon the good through which we attain something better."

No situation is entirely good or evil. In the concrete there exists always some mixture of truth and falsehood, joy and pain, growth and diminishment. We foster whatever is good, while striving to our utmost to resist whatever is evil in any given situation. In order to receive the full good intended by God, we undergo patiently our dark night, letting God produce his salvific effect through it.[6]

Through the cross, God actually accomplishes a greater good for us than had we not had to suffer. God quite literally "converts everything into good for those who love him" (*Rm* 8:28). This "good" is transforming union with God himself, eternal life, everlasting love and happiness. "What we suffer here is not even worthy of being compared to the glory which is coming...in Christ Jesus our Lord (*Rm* 8:18, 39).[7]

Through patient endurance God opens us to the good which is deeper than the evil so that we may arrive at what is truly better.

Both the spiritual director and the directee exercise most assuredly a great deal of patience towards each other. The director bears patiently the directee's laxity, sinfulness, reluctance to face the truth, defense mechanisms, etc. The director bears patiently also his/her own shortcomings which emerge in interaction with the directee: selfishness, bias, tension, impetuosity, etc. Needless to say, the directee frequently has much to put up with in the director: for instance, drowsiness, inattentiveness, stubbornness.

[5]See *Receptivity*, pp. 85-103.
[6]See *Receptivity*, pp. 32-53, 114-121.
[7]See *Receptivity*, pp. 96-97, 106-109.

Furthermore, both the director and the directee need to be patient with God. Or, to put it more precisely: They must be patient with their own impatience towards God and his mysterious ways.

While there are certain thresholds in the process of transformation which are universally applicable, the specific way in which God transforms each person into his likeness is wholly unique. We need to endure with patience God's painstaking manner of transforming and purifying. We have to wait patiently for him to effect our spiritualization. We cannot at our own initiative accelerate the growth process. Transformation takes a lifetime. So, "await patiently the presence of the Lord: Learn from the farmer. He waits for the precious fruit.... He waits patiently for the autumn and spring rains. You too must be longsuffering and stand firm, because the presence of the Lord is at hand" (*Jm* 5:7-8).

Patience allows the burden of what we undergo to be lightened and kept in perspective. Impatience, on the other hand, never improves effectively a situation. It produces only increased tension, dissipation and frustration.


## C. Truthfulness

"Love rejoices in the truth" (1 *Co* 13:6).

The truth is that which corresponds to reality, to what actually is. Truthfulness is, therefore, the interior attitude which acknowledges what is real, accepts it and seeks to live accordingly.

If you abide in truth, "truth will make you free" (*Jn* 8:32). But evangelical truth is not only the teaching of Jesus. It is especially the person of Christ himself: "I am the Truth" (*Jn* 14:6). Thus, "if the Son sets you free, you will be free indeed" (*Jn* 8:36).

Truthfulness or honesty is a necessary disposition of one abiding in the truth. We can never really listen to God or to anyone else until we are free enough to embrace the whole truth of ourselves in God and of God in us. Therein lies the rub: How much truth can we stand? How much truth do we really want to know?

Truth is far more experiential than cognitive. Yes, we assent to truth, we know truth, we acknowledge truth. We believe Jesus. But we must do/be more: We must especially believe *in* Christ. Then we shall believe *in* the Truth by means of the "Spirit of truth" dwelling in us (*Jn* 14:17).

Enabling us to abide in Christ who is Truth incarnate, the Spirit of truth reveals to our minds and hearts the particular truths necessary at any given time to open us more to infinite truth. For instance, God reveals to us some dimension of self-knowledge, some aspect of a call to a particular ministry, some directive which we are to follow.

As directors we help the directee remain receptive to these particular truths as well as to truth in itself. Through our words and silence, challenges and encouragement, corrections and advice, the Spirit from within the directee awakens his/her consciousness to truth. The directee thus penetrates ever more deeply into the unfathomable depths of God within him/herself and within the world.

In response to the directee's disclosures and to God's inspiration, the director must be always candid and straightforward in giving counsel, instruction and encouragement. This necessity for truthfulness is especially evident in situations requiring confrontation.

By confrontation we mean direct exposure of a person's inner poverty. Usually this exposure occurs in a context in which the directee is either consciously or unconsciously avoiding or resisting the truth. This avoidance or resistance need not imply ill will, although often it does presuppose formidable defense mechanisms. To confront means to face head-on, to challenge, to encounter.

Confrontation is an honest effort to help the directee see and work through the obstacles to transformation in God. It is a means of opening the directee to greater self-knowledge and self-acceptance by pointing out the inconsistencies of his/her behavior in relation to his/her inner thrust. What one is ultimately confronted with is the depth of one's poverty together with the impossibility of being able to do anything about it, except in total surrender to Christ Jesus our Lord (*Rm* 7:14-25).

In order that confrontation be helpful for the directee, it must be inspired by the Spirit of truth. Confrontation is always painful and difficult for both the director and directee. Some directors are more aggressive by nature, others more shy. Some are more intense, others more reserved. Some directees are more sensitive by nature, others more accepting. In all instances confrontation hurts to some degree.

Our manner of confronting should communicate sensitivity and compassion. Salvific confrontation springs from a desire for growth. Building upon an already existing rapport of confidence and trust, we convey to the directee our continued encouragement throughout and after the confrontation.

When inclined to confront, the director needs to discern the origin of the impulse. If it originates primarily in ourselves, the inclination to confront can be triggered by impatience, fatigue, stress, aggressivity, anger, desire to control. If it is from the Spirit, then it flows readily out of the discernment process.

Frequently, the director faces situations wherein mixed motives are at play: some arising from the Spirit, others originating in self. In these instances the director discerns and acts upon the more dominant influence.

At times the director has no choice but to confront. In fact, the confrontational approach is normally the last resort. Occasionally, however, the director does have alternatives such as letting the matter go a while longer or trying more indirect approaches such as posing questions and making suggestions. Having carefully weighed his/her motivation as well as the alternatives and the probable consequences of his/her actions, only the director can decide in each case whether confrontation is appropriate.

When confrontation seems called for, the long-range spiritual ill effects of not going through with it far outweigh the immediate emotional pain and hurt of implementing it.

Jesus himself never hesitated to confront when necessary. He never feared to let the pieces fall where they would. Jesus confronted his enemies: the scribes, the Pharisees (*Mt* 23), the chief priests and the whole Sanhedrin (*Jn* 18:19-24) and Pilate (*Jn* 18:33-38). He confronted his friends: Philip (*Jn* 14:8-9), Thomas (*Jn* 20: 24-29) and Peter several times (*Mk* 8:31-33; *Lk* 22:31-34; *Jn* 18:10-11). He confronted even his own mother (*Lk* 2:49; *Jn* 2:4) and his own emotions (*Lk* 22:41-44; *Jn* 12:27-28). St. Paul was not one to shy away from confrontation either: with the Corinthians (almost every chapter of 1 and 2 *Co* in one form or another), with Peter (*Ga* 2:11-14), with Philemon (*Phm* 8-21), etc.

As directors we have to examine carefully any hesitancy to confront. Does reluctance arise from the fact that confrontation is truly inappropriate at least at this time? Or, does it spring from fear of being wrong, fear of rejection, fear of hurting the directee or of being hurt ourselves? Hesitancy to confront may also stem from lack of trust in God, personal complacency and conflict of interest. Conflicts of interest between the spiritual good of the directee and the less-than-spiritual goods of the director are more common than one might suspect. Emotional attachment or its opposite leads to formidable conflicts of interest. The possibility of financial gain or loss to oneself or one's community is another source of conflict.

In confrontation, we should consider just how much truth a directee can sustain at a given time. The only purpose of confrontation is to build upon the truth. We are not to "break the crushed reed, or quench the wavering flame" (*Is* 42:3). No, especially in confrontation we are called 'to open the eyes of the blind, to free captives from prison, and those who live in darkness from the dungeon" (*Is* 42:7). Frequently, a perceptive director sees much more than is prudent to reveal all at once to the directee. Even God does not reveal to us in one fell swoop all the bitter truth about ourselves. He quite literally takes a lifetime.

Timing is a crucial ingredient in confrontation. "Unto everything there is a season" (*Qo* 3:1). When it is God's time the directee will, despite initial anger and resistance, be ready interiorly to undergo the truth. If, however, the director acts rashly or prematurely, confrontation can be a devastating experience for the directee. Instead of opening the directee more to God, confrontation can backfire with the result that the directee further intensifies his/her defensive mechanisms and thus becomes even more alienated from self, God and others.

There is always risk involved in using confrontation. Yet, should we discern to the best of our ability that it is necessary, we must proceed in faith. God will not fail to use it somehow for the good of the directee (*Rm* 8:28, 31, 37-39).

Truthfulness requires that the director be free from self-seeking. "Faithfully s/he brings true justice" (*Is* 42:3-4. Truth is not always welcomed immediately by those to whom it is proclaimed. Unconcerned with gaining human praise or respect, the director must seek only the approval that comes from God. "As for human glory, this means nothing to me....How can you believe since you receive glory from one another and you do not seek glory from the one God?" (*Jn* 5:41, 44).

## D. *Gentleness*

"Love is gentle.... Love does not delight in evil" (1 *Co* 13:4, 6).

Truthfulness in listening needs to be balanced with gentleness, meekness, kindness, compassion. Gentleness is always important in spiritual direction. It is crucial when confrontation is required. "If one of you sins, you who are spiritual should set him/her straight in a spirit of gentleness, not forgetting that you yourselves are also prone to temptation" (*Ga* 6:1). "A servant of the Lord must be kind and forbearing towards everyone.... With gentleness s/he instructs those who oppose him/her, never forgetting that God may give them a change of heart so that they may come to full knowledge of the truth" (2 *Tm* 2:24-25).

Gentleness is a quality of being. True, a person may *act* with kindness. But that is so only because that person *is* gentle, meek, compassionate. Gentleness is something intangible. It permeates every aspect of the director's stance towards the directee. Gentleness expresses empathy with the weakness of the other. The intensity of this gentleness and consequent empathy corresponds to the director's own experience of his/her personal sinfulness and weakness. Gentleness intensifies as we mellow throughout the course of our life struggle.

The director manifests gentleness by remaining sensitive to and compassionate with the frailty and vulnerability of the directee. The gentle director imitates the servant of Yahweh: "He does not cry out or raise his voice.... He does not break the crushed reed, or quench the wavering flame" (*Is* 42:2-3). That is, holding sacred the vulnerability of the directee, the director builds on the most subtle receptivity.

Through the meekness of the director, the directee experiences something of the gentleness of God's love. God's love is everlasting (*Ps* 100: 5). It is infinitely merciful and compassionate. It is always faithful. Through the experience of God's gentle love, the directee in turn learns to be more gentle with him/herself as well as with others.

Origen advises persons seeking spiritual direction: "First, test the physician before you open yourself to him. Determine whether he can be ill with one who is ill, weep with one who weeps. See whether he imparts instruction with gentleness and forbearance."[8]

St. Basil admonishes: The spiritual director "must care for weak souls with tenderness and humility of heart.... He must be compassionate and long-suffering with those who through inexperience fall short in duty. He should not pass over their sins in silence, but must bear gently with the sinner, applying remedies in all kindness and moderation."[9]

---

[8]*Hom. 2 on Ps. 37* (*PG*, 12:1386).
[9]*The Long Rules*, 43 (*PG*, 31:1027-1030).

## E. Competency

"Love does not boast. It is not proud" (1 *Co* 13:4).

In addition to the preceding qualities, competency in ascetical-mystical theology is essential in exercising the ministry of spiritual direction. The director not only *lives* an intense "life in faith" (*Ga* 2:20), but also seeks to understand deeply this same faith. Every spiritual director needs to ponder with heart and mind the mysteries of salvation.[10]

Competency in ascetical-mystical theology is acquired through two principal sources: (1) by personal reflection on our own faith experience as well as that of our directees, and (2) by indepth study of the scriptures, spirituality, patrology, history as well as sufficient exposure to systematic theology.

Although he emphasizes the importance of the director's faith experience, St. John of the Cross insists also on theological competency: "The fundamental requirement for a spiritual guide is knowledge and ability to discern. Yet, if s/he does not have experience of what is pure and truly spiritual, s/he will never be able to direct a soul therein or even to understand it."[11]

Lamenting the theological incompetency of so many directors, John continues, "Such persons do not know what spirit means. They perpetrate great insult and irreverence by putting their clumsy hand where God is working.... Perhaps these directors mean well, but they err through insufficient knowledge. Yet this is no excuse for the advice they so rashly give without first understanding either the way the soul is taking or its spirit."[12]

St. Teresa of Jesus, reflecting on her own experience of being directed by others, also stresses the necessity of theological competency: "I have always been attracted by learn-

[10]See *Contemplation*, pp. 131-133.

[11]*Flame*, 3, 30.

[12]*Flame*, 3, 54, 56.

ing. But confessors with only a little learning have done my soul great harm. I have not always found persons who had as much learning as I would have liked. I have discovered by experience that if these confessors are virtuous and lead holy lives it is better that they should have no theology at all than have only a little. For it they had none at all, they would not trust themselves (nor would I myself trust them) unless they first consulted others who were really learned. A truly learned confessor has never led me astray. It is not that these others deliberately meant to misguide me. They simply did not know any better."[13]

They were ignorant, but did not know it.

Once the director has sufficient theological background, one excellent approach to continuing the study of the process of spiritualization is prolonged, indepth study of the life and spirituality of a personally chosen spiritual master. Some examples are: St. Paul, St. Augustine, St. John of the Cross, St. Teresa of Jesus, St. Francis of Assisi, St. Francis de Sales, Pierre Teilhard de Chardin, Thomas Merton to mention only a few.

The criterion to follow in selecting such an author is this: We should choose someone to whom we are intuitively drawn. The experience of an affinity towards a particular master indicates ordinarily that certain aspects of that author's process of transformation in God bears resemblance to our own. Thus, this study, besides being intellectual, has also an experiential quality about it. It is a veritable undergoing with another the experience of Christ.

Throughout the course of this study (which may take years, even decades) we discover, while transcending the peculiarities of the author's personality and times, principles of discernment which are universally applicable. For instance, we discover signs which indicate the presence of the night of sense, the beginning of contemplation, the night of spirit, the thresholds which are crossed in the more advanced stages of transforming union.

[13] *Life*, 5.

In addition to competency in ascetical-mystical theology, a working knowledge of the basic principles of psychology is important. This enables the director to recognize when to refer a directee for counseling on therapy. A basic knowledge of psychology aids also in taking a more holistic approach to the directee's needs, especially in the area of emotional turbulence arising from deep hurts, anger, bereavement, etc. Furthermore, a knowledge of some psychology helps us identify latent difficulties in communicating with the directee, difficulties which obstruct the listening process.

Spiritual direction encompasses all the interior and exterior dimensions of a directee's life. Moreover, these are situated within the broader perspective of the world's pursuits, endeavors, struggles and aspirations. To assist the directee more fully, the director needs to consider this broader milieu in which the directee is immersed. To this end, some awareness of current events which are of social, historical or religious significance is necessary. In order to read the signs of the times we must first have sufficient familiarity with the times themselves.

This does not imply that the director is to reinforce the values, standards, or ways of the world. Quite the contrary. The director's essential role is to affirm and proclaim the way in which God is becoming all in all within the world (1 *Co* 15:28), while at the same time protesting against anything contrary to this transformation. The authentic spiritual director is eminently a prophet.

In the act of listening to God within a directee, the director does not usually rely directly on acquired knowledge of any kind — be it theology, psychology or current events. Yet, such knowledge, even though not directly adverted to, does help to open us to the direction that the Spirit is indicating. Acquired knowledge increases also our ability to help the directee translate into consciousness something of his/her existential experience of the mystery of Christ.

*Chapter 12*

# The Spiritual Director-Directee Relationship

The personal relationship between the director and the directee constitutes the context in which all interaction between them transpires. It is also the medium through which most divine communication is effected. "The first thing," therefore, "that genuine spiritual direction requires in order to work properly is a normal, spontaneous human relationship."[1]

## A. The Relationship as Interpersonal

Especially at the outset, the director's mode of being toward the directee sets the tone for the unfolding of this interpersonal relationship.

As directors, we must above all be ourselves. This entails maintaining a stance of openness and receptivity, without defenses, pretense or affectation. We present ourselves as we are in our poverty and richness, in our strengths and weak-

---

[1]*S. Direction*, p. 11.

nesses. Interacting with the directee, we remain simple, sincere and truthful. We cannot hide behind a role in order to protect our vulnerability, nor can we fit ourselves into a role to accommodate the expectations or projections of the directee.

This ability to be ourselves presupposes basic self-knowledge and self-acceptance. We can be at ease with another only if we first accept ourselves in the many facets which constitute our personalities. The freedom to be ourselves springs from deep personal abandonment in faith to God and profound trust in the presence and guidance of his indwelling Spirit. The more intense our dependency on God becomes, the more simple, unpretentious and relaxed we remain.

To the extent that we can be ourselves, we become capable of being genuinely loving, caring and accepting towards the directee. While these qualities are obviously manifest in our gestures and words, they become particularly transparent in our mode of being and in our attitudes.

The ability to be ourselves reaps many benefits. It instills in the directee a sense of confidence and trust. This in turn encourages the directee to present him/herself as s/he is. Certainly, without the directee's willingness to be transparent before the director it is extremely difficult, if not impossible, for spiritual direction to emerge.

When the director and the directee remain themselves, spontaneity and creativity characterize their relationship. This spontaneity and creativity reflect the basic attitude of each towards God. These qualities witness unmistakably to a stance of loving receptivity to the Father, peaceful attentiveness to the Son, patient waiting upon the Spirit.

The spiritual director-directee relationship has both a transcendent and an immanent dimension. Not only do the director and the directee listen together to God who is Other than both of them, but also they wait together upon him who abides within each of them as well as within the relationship between them. "Where two or three are united in my name, there am I in their midst" (*Mt* 18:20).

The immanence of God is especially incarnate in the mutual love between the director and the directee. God loves each person in a singular manner. Therefore, the love with which he loves each directee in and through a director is unique. Likewise, the love with which God loves the director in and through each directee is unique. The director and the directee can abide in mutual love even when negative feelings, personality conflicts or confrontations arise.

In the encounter between director and directee, all aspects of their respective personalities come into play. These include not only what is deepest and most mysterious in each, but also their temperamental characteristics, idiosyncrasies, personal strengths and weaknesses.

Generally speaking, directors run the gamut of emotional reactions towards their directees. Towards a few we experience strong natural affinity, possibly even emotional attraction. We really like them. We look forward with eagerness and enthusiasm to seeing them. On the other hand, there are always a few whom we experience as psychic-drainers. Ten minutes with these persons wear us out. They are a chore, a burden. We may even dislike certain ones. We catch ourselves shortening their time, trying to get through the meeting as quickly as possible. We find ourselves prone to cancel their appointments under the slightest pretext. We do not like the way these persons talk, walk, dress. Their value systems and their outlook towards life may run counter to our own. Their idiosyncrasies irritate us. At times our emotional reactions are suggestive of latent or outright personality clash. Towards most of our directees, however, we experience emotional equanimity. Without tending towards either attraction or dislike, we find these persons affable, interesting and frequently challenging. We get along well with them when they are present, but we do not give them a second thought when they are gone.

Nonetheless, while it is normal to *feel* differently towards each directee, as directors we must maintain the same loving, respectful, listening attitude towards each. Regardless of personal preferences, we have to be willing to give each one our undivided attention and presence.

Directees also experience a myriad of emotional responses towards directors. These responses range anywhere from affection to dislike.

On a natural level, the director and the directee do not always correspond emotionally to each other. For example, a directee may have considerable affection for a director, who in turn may feel quite unaffected towards the same directee. Or, a director may experience deep concern and empathy for a directee who in turn is entertaining anger and resentment towards him/her.

Both the director and the directee must listen to what is transpiring in the interaction between them. They need to admit and accept their true feelings. Only thus can they work through any difficulties in communication. The recognition and the acceptance of these feelings go a long way towards lessening undue tension and stress in the relationship. This honesty tends also to minimize the negative effects inordinate feelings have on the listening process. Even strong natural attraction or feelings of dislike can be coped with, provided both the director and the directee are called together by God. God never demands the impossible.

Mutual feelings of attraction and mutual feelings of contrariness are handled best when both the director and the directee together confront their feelings for each other. This is especially advisable when the relationship promises to be of long duration. Clearing the air in this manner lessens excessive emotional tension.

Yet, sometimes the feelings are not mutual. In this case, it may still be appropriate for the directee to discuss his/her feelings towards the director, especially if this pertains to the manifestation of the heart. However, it is seldom, if ever, advisable for a director to discuss his/her true feelings towards the directee when their feelings for each other are not mutual. If a director is emotionally attracted to a certain directee who is not likewise attracted towards him/her, this disclosure only disquiets the directee, and serves no positive purpose. On the other hand, if a director is repelled by certain mannerisms of the directee who has confidence and trust in him/her, such a disclosure could crush the directee and impede further openness. In these instances, the director should get a handle on his/her emotional reactions, and quietly transcend them.

## B. Emotional Attraction

Emotional attraction between the director and the directee can pose certain obvious difficulties. These difficulties are substantially the same whether the relationship is with a member of the same or the opposite sex. The emotional attraction may occur in one of three contexts: (1) that of a mature directee and an immature director, (2) that of an immature directee and a mature director, and (3) that of a mature directee and a mature director.

In the case where both are immature, the director-directee relationship should cease immediately. If not, they will both fall into the same pit (*Mt* 15:14). In this instance, the relationship could be resumed only if the immaturity of at least one of the two was overcome. If in addition to being immature both are also insincere, the spiritual director-directee relationship in the strict sense cannot exist, since neither is searching for God.

### (1) A MATURE DIRECTEE AND AN IMMATURE DIRECTOR

In our supposition, the director may or may not be sincere about what is taking place. Nonetheless, discovering him-/herself the object of the directee's affection, the director handles the matter imprudently and immaturely either because of naivete or self-indulgence.

The director, for instance, may be inexperienced in affective relationships. S/he may find him/herself drifting in the direction of increasing affective involvement with the directee. If the director is a sincere person, s/he will eventually come to his/her senses, and take the appropriate action. If, on the other hand, the director is insincere, s/he will rationalize what is happening or even directly manipulate the developing affection for his/her own ends.

The directee, though sincere in this relationship, may also be somewhat naive. Holding the director in high esteem and believing the director to be holy and wise, the directee may be tempted to follow the director's initiative. Yet, if the developing relationship is really incompatible with growth in the Spirit, the intuition and common sense of a sincere directee eventually wins out.

Situations similar to the above arise in contexts other than those which are specifically affective. Subjugation is an example. An immature director, usually a man, may need to subjugate a directee, usually a woman, to his power. He may exercise such control over her that she has little will of her own. It is one thing to submit in faith to the advice of one's director. It is quite another to sell one's soul to him.

## (2) AN IMMATURE DIRECTEE AND A MATURE DIRECTOR

Some directees try to manipulate the relationship in a manner which is incompatible with the director's commitment to God and love for them. Basically insincere directees who experience a strong affection or physical attraction for their director may actually set out to seduce the director. They may use elaborate rationalization to convince themselves and their director that they are indeed sincere.

This tendency to seduce is sometimes very clever. For example, a directee reveals to the director an attraction for him/her. But the matter does not stop there. The directee insists on discussing these feelings week after week. S/he claims this is necessary in order to learn to deal with the affection more maturely. Yet, the real purpose for this repeated and prolonged discussion is to contrive a reciprocal response from the director.

To this end, the directee may engage in double talk. Suppose the directee makes a statement to this effect: "I get scared sometimes and wonder how you can possibly care for me." On the surface it sounds as if the directee is trying to come to terms with a poor self-image. Yet, in reality this may be a leading statement encouraging the director to respond in this manner: "Don't worry. Of course I care for you. I love you just as you love me." The director means this response in one sense. The directee takes it in quite another. S/he latches on to all the director's affirming remarks and distorts them to suit his/her twisted purposes. Affirmations by the director feed this person's daydreaming and phantasizing, thereby building up unrealistic hopes. This directee may be unable to grasp the fact, even when it is explicitly stated, that the director has not responded in the sense that s/he interpreted it.

How does the director handle constructively situations such as this one? First of all, the director has to recognize the problem for what it is. Unless s/he sees through the directee's ploys, the director falls blindly into them. The directee then has the power to manipulate and to control the director in practically any way s/he chooses.

The director should challenge the directee to examine honestly his/her immaturities and to accept the truth of his/her feelings and behavior. Unless there is some indication that a directee can live with and grow beyond these feelings, the relationship cannot continue. If necessary, the director may have to state categorically that s/he is not available for the kind of relationship that the directee desires.

Resoluteness and consistency are necessary on the part of the director. S/he cannot afford to send out ambivalent signals to an immature, infatuated directee. The director cannot be firm one moment, and joke or socialize the next.

## (3) A MATURE DIRECTEE AND A MATURE DIRECTOR

Genuine love, appreciation and gratitude are normal fruits of a sincere and mature relationship in the Spirit. Yet frequently, because they are so sincere directees become anxious lest their affection for their director develop contrary to their commitment to God. The same can be said of directors towards directees.

St. Teresa of Jesus observed a similar problem among her nuns: "If persons who are practicing prayer find that their confessor is a holy man and understands God's way in them, they become greatly attracted to him. And immediately they are beseiged by a whole battery of scruples which produce a terrible disturbance within them."[2]

The directee in this situation may even consider changing directors. Should s/he do so, however, the same concern will likely recur: "If the confessor is guiding such persons to greater perfection, they become so distraught over their attraction to him that they will go so far as to leave him for another and yet another, only to be tormented by the same temptation every time." Teresa goes on to offer this jewel of advice: "What you should do in this situation is not to let yourselves dwell on whether you like your confessor or not. Go ahead and be attracted to him if you feel so inclined."[3]

A directee must never deny or repress his/her affection. It is not possible to enter into a genuine spiritual friendship without some emotional attachment, at least initially. We are sexual, feeling beings. So, this side of death all human affection entails necessarily a sexual dimension which may range anywhere from pleasant-to-be-with to considerable physical attraction. All this can be quite normal and healthy. Consequently, it should not receive more attention than it deserves. There is no reason to become preoccupied with it.

The directee should follow this counsel: If you experience affection for your director, let it be. Go ahead and love him/her in a manner that befits the relationship itself, together with your respective vocations and commitments. Love your director as Jesus loves you and as the Father is inviting you to love. How can we not love those who incarnate God's love for us?

---

[2] *Way of Perfection*, BAC 3rd ed. 7, 2. (Peers, trans., Image D176, p. 60).
[3] *Ibidem* (p. 60).

An affection of this nature may greatly benefit the directee in the process of spiritualization: "If we grow fond of people who are kind to our bodies, why should we not love those who strive so hard to help our souls? If my confessor is a holy and spiritual man, and I see that he is taking great pains for the benefit of my soul, I think that being attracted to him would help my progress. We are so weak that such affection sometimes helps us to undertake important works in God's service."[4]

Even when both director and directee are sincere about their relationship, their mutual affection may contain initially elements of immaturity and selfishness. With time the Spirit gradually perfects and purifies their love in a more spiritual direction. "In the beginning, love may not be perfect, but the Lord will make it increasingly so....At first, it may be mingled with emotion, but this as a rule does no harm. It is sometimes good and necessary for us to show emotion in our love and also to feel it."[5]

The relationship between the director and the directee is itself in a continuous, although often gradual, process of spiritualization. Thus, there is an ongoing relativization of what both may have thought would remain permanent in their affection. They may have assumed that their love and their manner of interaction would always remain as it had existed in the beginning. Yet, they discover that this passes away gradually as a more spiritual mode of loving and relating emerges.

## C. Dependence, Independence, Interdependence

The directee who begins spiritual direction at a relatively early stage of interior development and who continues it for many years normally passes through three basic phases in relationship to the director (or directors, since one may have

[4]*Ibidem* (p. 60-61).
[5]*Ibidem* (p. 76).

several in the course of a lifetime). The directee grows gradually from dependence on a director to increasing independence. This latter, with time and further maturity, evolves into an interdependence.

Reliance on the director in the initial phases of spiritual direction does not necessarily imply that the directee shirks assuming personal responsibility for choices or decisions. Such behavior would suggest a dependency which is obviously immature. We are speaking rather of a mature dependency in which the directee relies on the director as a special instrument through whom the Spirit awakens consciousness to God's direction being formed within him/her. The directee thus realizes that human assistance is needed in order to discover God's particular design. A beginner usually has to see the director on a frequent and regular basis. This necessity may last for quite some time.

The directee must first increase so that Christ can increase.[6] The director therefore helps the neophyte build up a strong self for Christ.

In so doing, the director cannot shelter the directee from life. We encourage the directee's interaction with peers, family, community, colleagues and authority. We remain open to receive from others any valid observations or constructive criticism that may be of assistance in guiding the directee. Sometimes, we have to even seek out another informed opinion with respect to the directee.

At the outset, we help the directee discern which lifestyle is compatible with his/her inner direction. We offer also practical assistance in setting the directee on the proper course towards an integrated prayer life.

It is not unusual to see the directee begin imitating in these initial phases certain aspects of the director's personal spirituality. This is healthy provided that the directee can distinguish between what is interiorly meaningful and what is foreign to his/her innate spiritual thrust.

---

[6]See *D. Milieu*, pp. 49-73; *Contemplation*, pp. 118-119; *Receptivity*, pp. 83-88.

In building up a strong self for Christ, however, the directee soon comes to perceive that s/he cannot continue indefinitely in this direction. As a logical development of this effort, s/he experiences a desire to surrender more deeply to God, to be abandoned in love and dark faith to him. The directee realizes inexorably that henceforth s/he must decrease so that Christ can further increase (*Jn* 3:30).[7]

At this threshold of spiritual development we foster in the directee maximum receptivity to God's transforming and purifying love. We help the directee identify and dispel any illusions and encourage him/her to continue the journey in deeper faith, hope and love.

Gradually the directee moves away from former reliance on the director towards independence. S/he becomes emancipated. The directee begins to experience spiritual direction sometimes as meaningful and at other times as unnecessary. Sessions with the director become fewer and farther apart.

At this phase, ambivalence sometimes creeps into the directee's attitude towards the relationship with the director. On the one hand, with emerging spiritual maturity the directee becomes increasingly capable of discerning more independently. On the other hand, the directee is not yet mature enough to discern consistently without some assistance. Thus, even though the directee generally acts more independently of a director there are still occasions when s/he relies specifically on a director's guidance.

When the directee does seek help from us, we should be readily available, offering whatever support, encouragement and guidance the Spirit desires. Nonetheless, we must not use these occasions to attempt to reestablish the rapport which characterized an earlier phase of the relationship. Instead, we explicitly encourage the directee in his/her movement towards greater emancipation. We let the directee go, allowing him/her the freedom to respond as independently as the Spirit leads.

---

[7]See *D. Milieu*, pp. 74-111; *Contemplation*, pp. 118-121; *Receptivity*, 83-85, 89-103.

Once the directee becomes consistently capable of discerning his/her spiritual direction without direct assistance, we discover the relationship at another threshold: that of interdependence.

The phase of interdependence is characterized by equality. As far as discernment is concerned, the director and the directee are peers. They stand before each other as spiritual persons on equal footing. Meetings become rare. Words are few. Yet, as each silently, mysteriously lives in the one Spirit, the Spirit draws them ever more into the life of God. "Draw me in your footsteps. Let us run together" (*Sg* 1:4). Their rapport and dependence converge more and more directly in God, and in him they encounter one another more fully. They become interdependent in God.

Throughout the relationship, God has increasingly purified their love. In God, the director now beholds in mystery the life that the Spirit has released in the directee. In God also, the directee beholds with gratitude and boundless appreciation the spiritual guide who has been so instrumental in his/her spiritualization. However, this is still not the end of the journey. Each continues to search and grow in loving adoration of Father, Son and Spirit.

The length of time necessary for these phases to mature as well as the specific manner in which a given relationship evolves is entirely the "Father's business" (*Lk* 2:49). These particulars depend on God's activity within both the director and the directee. Usually, any number of obstacles arise which slow down or impede temporarily the spiritualization of the relationship. But if the relationship itself is destined by God, he will not let any weakness of ours effectively thwart his will (*Is* 55: 10-11; *Rm* 8:31). "He who began this good work in" us "will bring it to completion on the day of Christ Jesus" (*Ph* 1:6).

When a more spiritually mature directee seeks out a director, their relationship need not pass through the whole process described above. Frequently, such a relationship begins at the phase of independence or even at that of interdependence.

A director crosses paths with many directees for brief intervals. Some need help only in time of a particular crisis, others during a directed retreat or for a period of a few weeks or months. In these cases, the thresholds of the relationship we have been describing do not usually have time to develop.

## D. Specific Questions

Certain aspects of the spiritual director-directee relationship require special consideration. These are confidentiality, obedience and change of director.

### (1) CONFIDENTIALITY

Out of respect for the mystery of God and for the directee's personal right to privacy, the spiritual director is bound to keep confidential all disclosures.

Strict confidentiality quite naturally tends to increase the directee's sense of trust and security. This trust in turn fosters openness and frankness with respect to all inner struggles, even those which are a source of embarrassment.

In order to discern better with the directee, the director may need to consult another person on occasion. The situation may require a second opinion. This consultation could include another experienced director, the directee's spouse or major superior, the directee's psychiatrist, confidant or close friend. Generally speaking, such consultation should take place only with the directee's *prior* knowledge and consent. The only instance in which prior consent might not be required is when common sense indicates that implicit consent already exists and that the director could legitimately presume explicit consent were the directee available to grant it. In these cases, only what is necessary should be revealed about the directee during the consultation. Moreover, the directee must always be advised post factum that the consultation has taken place. When there is doubt about the existence of implicit consent on the part of the directee, the director must always act in favor of strict confidentiality. Consultation should not be made as long as the doubt persists.

The principle of confidentiality on the part of the director is well recognized. However, what is frequently overlooked is the fact that the directee also has a serious corresponding responsibility. The directee is bound to use discretion with regard to all spiritual advice received from the director.

Advice given by a director is meant for a specific directee in very particular circumstances. Because each person's journey to the Father is so unique, what is appropriate for one individual may be detrimental for another. It is, therefore, irresponsible and imprudent for a directee to indiscriminately pass on to friends and acquaintances directives received from a spiritual guide.

The directee has of course every right to seek another's advice. The director may even suggest consultation. But if a directee consults another, with or without the director's consent, in all fairness to the director and in honesty to this relationship the directee should advise him/her of this fact. Furthermore, in the act of consultation with another, the directee is bound in conscience to reveal as accurately as possible the whole context in which the director has issued a given directive. To proceed otherwise would be to manipulate the consultation for one's own ends.

A directee can be especially prone to breach confidentiality in a situation of conflict with the director. Angry and upset, the directee seeks out someone for sympathy and consolation. The directee then proceeds to reveal only those elements of the conflict which serve his/her purpose. S/he gives a one-sided account colored by prejudice and hurt. Such behavior is obviously self-serving and sometimes vengeful.

This behavior can have harmful effects for both the director and the directee. In misrepresenting the situation the directee presents a negative image of the director. Damage to the director's reputation may result. Without even knowing the director, others judge him/her on the basis of the directee's prejudiced disclosures.

Furthermore, blabbering about the difficulties with the director usually brings upon the directee unnecessary suffering. Naturally, there are times when a directee must work through negative feelings or resistance. This is part of the spiritual direction process. However, another person may mistakenly encourage the directee in thinking that the director misunderstands or is not acting in his/her best interests. This misguided advice retards or even blocks the emergence of direction and further reinforces the directee's defense mechanisms.

The directee must have trust and faith in the director. Together they have to continue listening and searching despite their conflict. "If there is some point on which you disagree, God will reveal to you the appropriate way" (*Ph* 3:15).

When a directee becomes upset with the director or unsatisfied with what is emerging as spiritual direction, s/he must bear this pain trustfully and patiently. Certainly the directee has to recognize and accept his/her feelings, without in any way denying or repressing them. Nevertheless, these are to be discussed only in a proper context: that is, either with the director or with a neutral party who is given a *full* account of the conflict. Outside of this proper context, the directee should undergo his/her struggle in silence or else change directors altogether, if s/he is truly desirous of spiritual direction.

## (2) OBEDIENCE

For any follower of Jesus, obedience to the Father is basic to all spiritual genesis (*Jn* 4:34). There is nothing more fundamental to authentic interior life than faith in God and unreserved abandonment to his will. So, obedience — complete surrender of oneself — to the Father is essential in spiritual direction.

But the question remains: To what extent does a directee owe obedience to the director?

This question has been disputed throughout the history of spirituality. Authors following the Thomistic tradition tend to replace the obligation of obedience to one's director with docility towards and prudent acceptance of his/her directives. Others following more specifically the Ignatian and Salesian traditions tend to insist on strict obedience to one's director.

For ourselves, we prefer to approach the question of obedience from a biblical perspective. The Hebrew scriptures render obeying as *shama*: listening. So also the New Testament speaks of obeying in terms of *hypakouo*: listening (literally, to listen under). Even the Latin word for *oboedire*, from which the English "obey" is derived, means "to listen to."

Thus, obedience in spiritual direction means listening to God and acting upon his word insofar as it is revealed through the director. Obedience denotes first and foremost listening to our Abba-Father, to his word and to his special instrument: the director. Then, having listened, the directee submits humbly to God and acts upon his word received through the director. Without obedience in this sense spiritual direction would be futile and the director-directee relationship a sham.

In the desert tradition, the biblical sense of obedience in spiritual direction is brought out strikingly in this simple logion: "Some brothers...visited Abba Felix. They implored him to speak a word. The old man, however, remained silent. After they repeated their request several times, he said, 'So you want to listen to a word, do you?' They replied, 'Yes, Abba, we do.' The old man continued: 'There are no more words nowadays. When the brothers and sisters used to consult the elders, they put into practice what was spoken. So, God gave words to the elders. But now, since the brothers and sisters ask without carrying out what they have listened to, God has withdrawn the gift of his word from the elders. They do not find anything to say, because there are no longer those who carry out their words."[8]

[8] *PG*, 65, 434 (24); *Sayings*, p. 202.

Merton interprets obedience in the desert tradition thus: "This is not blind, unreasoning and passive obedience of one who obeys merely in order to let himself be 'broken,' but the clear-sighted trusting obedience of one who firmly believes that his guide knows the true way to peace and purity of heart and is an interpreter of God's will for him."[9]

Usually, a directee can immediately identify and accept a particular directive as being expressive of a God-given insight. Sometimes, a directee may be able to follow the director's advice only after much struggle and resistance. On occasion, the Spirit within the directee moves him/her to submit in dark faith to the advice received, even though the directee cannot at that moment see the particular direction as coming from the Spirit. Rarely, the directee may have to reject, after careful discernment and in obedience to God, a certain directive as being incompatible with life in the Spirit.

## (3) CHANGE OF DIRECTOR

While remaining open to all the different ways through which God indicates spiritual direction, a directee should have, generally speaking, only one spiritual director at any given time. A directee may on occasion have more than one director, but this would occur under special circumstances: for example, during a directed retreat or some particular crisis. In these instances, the second director would be temporary and in a very specific context.

At times, the director and directee need to consult a third party in the discernment. This is usually the case when the director is unable to read the signs or when a serious conflict develops. The directee should refrain however, from needlessly consulting an endless stream of directors. There are persons who seem to be compulsive director-hoppers. They flit from one director to another and back again like bees in a flower garden. This behavior certainly throws into question the sincerity and the underlying emotional stability of

[9]*S. Father*, p. 301. See *S. Direction*, p. 40.

these directees. Often such directees reveal only certain spiritual experiences in a vain attempt to receive praise and esteem. Frequently, they try to escape from truth by choosing only what they want to hear out of the myriad of opinions which are offered. Furthermore, the advice of any director who challenges their illusion and egocentricity is quickly dismissed, since these directees can always find someone to side with them.

A change in geographical location for either the director or the directee can necessitate the termination of the relationship. In this instance, should the directee still need frequent, regular direction, it is best to seek another competent director in the immediate area.

Although direction can be pursued through correspondence, this mode of communication contains many limitations. Letter writing makes it difficult for both the directee and the director to express themselves in a way that is not open to misunderstanding. One may have much less facility and time than the other in corresponding. When misinterpretation does occur, immediate rectification of the matter is not always possible. By the time a response is received from the director, the circumstances and interior disposition of the directee may have altered considerably. The advice is therefore no longer apropos.

Perhaps the greatest drawback with direction by mail is the lack of personal contact. "In oral spiritual direction, much is communicated without words, even in spite of words. The direct person-to-person relationship is something that cannot be adequately replaced. Christ himself said, 'Where two or three are gathered together in my name, there am I in the midst of them.' There is a special spiritual presence of Christ in direct personal conversation, which guarantees a deeper and more intimate expression of the whole truth."[10]

If, however, infrequent meetings with the director suffice, geographical distance may not pose so great a difficulty.

[10] S. Direction, p. 39.

This assumes of course that the director already knows the directee sufficiently well. The director and directee may meet whenever possible. Between visits, the directee informs the director by correspondence of significant developments, with the director free to respond or not as the Spirit moves.

Occasionally, even though a directee still needs spiritual direction, the director after prayerful consideration may conclude that s/he has neither the wisdom nor the experience to guide the directee any further. The director must be honest with the directee, discuss terminating the relationship, and if possible recommend a more experienced person.

Other factors also lead the director to conclude that s/he is no longer of assistance to the directee. For example, the relationship becomes stagnant. The directee refuses to accept the guidance of the director and stubbornly goes his/her own way. Here, severing the relationship would come as a last resort, the director having patiently but unsuccessfully tried every other possible means to correct the situation.

On the other hand, the directee may consider terminating the relationship, even though there is still need for direction. Soon after entering into the relationship the directee senses, for instance, that s/he has made a mistake. Despite good will on the part of both, the directee cannot open up to the director in question. Or, after honest manifestation of the heart, the directee continues to experience misunderstanding on the part of the director.

The following principles help a directee discern whether or not to discontinue seeing a particular director.

(1) The directee should truthfully examine all motives for wanting to change directors. Is the desire to terminate this relationship a way of trying to escape the truth which God is revealing through my director? Is there a personality clash with my director? What factors am I aware of that may be preventing me from communicating with my director? Do I see him/her as an authority figure? Am I projecting negative qualities of authoritarianism, insensitivity, lack of understanding on my director? Do I have unrealistic expectations

of spiritual direction or of our relationship? Am I displeased with my director because s/he refuses to cater to my illusion or self-pity?

(2) The directee needs to discuss with the director the difficulties which s/he is experiencing in communication. Often a frank discussion can go a long way in resolving these problems.

(3) The directee must examine whether, in spite of the desire to discontinue, s/he is still receiving some spiritual benefit from the director's guidance. This may be a sign that at least for the present God wants the relationship to continue.

(4) The directee should explore the feasibility of changing directors. Is there another spiritual guide available to whom I am drawn? Am I drawn to this person for the proper reasons?.

(5) The directee has to avoid making a hasty or rash decision. S/he should give the whole question sufficient time and prayerful reflection.

(6) Before making a final decision, it is wise to discern the matter with a neutral party. "A change of director should be made only with prudent consideration, and if possible after consultation with a wise friend, a competent superior, or an alternate confessor."[11]

---

[11]*S. Direction*, p. 39.

## Chapter 13

# Listening and Poverty of Spirit

By poverty of spirit, we mean all our human limitations. These comprise our creatureliness, our sinfulness, our resistances, our passivities, our needs, our unfulfillments, our failures, our hurts, our frustrations, our disappointments. Poverty of spirit refers to everything in us which is not yet transformed in the likeness of the resurrected Christ (2 *Co* 3:18).

The ministry of spiritual direction affords spiritual directors a concrete and intense experience of their own inner poverty. In fact, vibrant within each of us there exists a dynamic interplay between the experience of personal limitation and the willingness to listen to God (*Rm* 7:14-25).

Confronted with the awesome responsibility of assisting directees discern their spiritual direction, we directors cannot but experience acutely our own poverty. Such a realization awakens us to the truth that "with human beings, this is impossible" (*Mk* 10:27). Yet, in poverty we turn to God in love, faith and hope, discovering equally that "with God, anything is possible" (*Mk* 10:27; *Lk* 1:37). The more we listen to God, the more we are driven to the awareness of our total dependency upon him. This awareness in turn opens us

further to listen more attentively to God. And so the interplay continues...

Our personal poverty becomes evident through a myriad
of ways: for instance, through inadequacy, self-sufficiency,
frustration, mistakes, vulnerability, the directee's poverty
and through the charism of spiritual direction itself.

## A. Inadequacy

As directors, we are confronted with the overwhelming
task of discovering God as he incarnates himself uniquely in
each directee entrusted to our care. Our spontaneous reaction is that of the sage: "What person can possibly know the
intentions of God? Who can conceivably divine the will of
the Lord? The reasonings of mortals are unsure; our intentions unstable" (*Ws* 9:13-14). And with St. Paul we confess:
"How impossible to penetrate God's motives or understand
his ways!" (*Rm* 11:33).

Our inner disposition must be one of receptivity. We enter
upon every encounter with each directee fully willing to let
go all our ways. There are occasions when either the directee
or we do have specific points in mind to discuss. Yet, we can
never predetermine the manner in which the discernment
will unfold. Nor can we ever entertain fixed ideas as to what
will ultimately emerge in listening. We must always be
willing to let the Spirit lead us along a way other than that
which we had originally intended.

St. Therese of the Child Jesus, herself a competent spiritual director, comments that "from a distance, doing good
for souls appears all roses: helping them love God more and
modeling them after one's own convictions. Yet at close
range, the experience is quite the opposite. The roses disap-
pear. One senses that to do well is almost as impossible
without God's assistance as making the sun shine at night....
One feels that it is absolutely necessary to abandon one's
likes, one's ideas, and guide souls uniquely by the way that

Jesus has traced out for them, without trying to force them to walk by one's own way."[1]

Throughout a given discernment process too, there are many moments of hesitation. We have no idea where we are heading. No perceptible insight is forthcoming. Furthermore, even when certain signs do appear we may not be immediately capable of interpreting them. Sometimes in complex issues, it may be quite difficult to know which aspects of the situation to focus on.

As directors, we enter into relationships with directees *as we are*. That means with our personal struggles, weaknesses and sinfulness as well as with our talents and gifts.

Interacting with our directees, we discover quickly our drawbacks as spiritual directors. Some directors hesitate to be truthful out of fear of rejection or of hurting their directees. Others are too blunt or categorical in the way that they confront. Unresolved hurts or personal problems prevent some directors from encouraging their directees to face courageously struggles similar to those in their own lives.

Conscious of their overwhelming poverty, directors question: Who am I to be guiding another, when there is still so much immaturity in me?

An inexperienced director may be especially haunted by feelings of inadequacy: I haven't studied enough. I haven't prayed enough. So and so is more knowledgeable or more prayerful. I'm too young, too inexperienced. In short, I just can't do it. I shouldn't venture where angels fear to tread.

When the director is not at peace acquiescing to mystery, a veritable interior panic occurs. This manifests itself in intense concern and stress centering around such gnawing questions as: What should I say? What should I do? Where do we go from here? How do we even get started? Am I doing what is right? The directee, perceiving the perplexity of the director, finds self-revelation increasingly difficult.

If God is really calling us to this ministry, no matter how inadequate we may think we are (or may actually be) God

---

[1] *Therese*, p. 238.

will not let that fact impede the accomplishment of his design (*Is* 55:10-11; *Jr* 1:6-8; *Rm* 8:28, 39). In such situations, directors need to recall these words of Yahweh: "My injunction for you today is not too difficult or beyond your grasp. . . . my word is very near to you. Indeed, it is in your mouth and within your heart. Therefore, obey it." (*Dt* 30:11-14).

## B. Self-Sufficiency

At the core of the above anxieties is usually a tendency to be self-reliant and self-centered. Certain directors want at least to appear confident and in control. Any tinge of self-sufficiency poses a formidable obstacle to listening. We do not have to *appear* any way at all. We do not have to seem wise, strong, disciplined, nor do we need to give the impression of being confused, weak or shifting either. To try to *appear* any way whatsoever is a mistake. We need only be ourselves, trusting in God who has begun this work and who himself will bring it to his desired completion (*Ph* 1:6). He can use our weaknesses for the good of the directee just as easily as he can use our strengths (2 *Co* 12:7-10). Even our deficiencies can be instruments of his grace. For example, a directee plagued with a bout of self-pity keeps whining and complaining. The director, frustrated and impatient, shouts: For heavens sake! Will you ever grow up? This remark, blurted out in exasperation, cuts the directee to the quick. But God uses it to shock the directee into realizing the depths of his/her self-centeredness.

Directors who are preoccupied with how they appear to their directees are usually mired down in self-analysis and introspection. Unsuccessful in their attempts to control the mystery of God, these directors become tense, frustrated and easily fatigued. Frequently, such persons persist in anger towards God for making things so difficult, towards themselves for all the interior turmoil that they cannot subdue (despite appearances possibly to the contrary), and towards the directee for supposedly having such high expectations for a perfect and all-wise director.

In letting us experience our powerlessness and poverty, God teaches each director this essential truth: You are not God. You are not anyone's savior. You are called to be God's instrument, his servant.

To assist the directee, therefore, we must as directors remain deeply receptive to God in all his mysteriousness. We have to abandon ourselves to God in the darkness of faith, intensely listening to him every moment along the way, always waiting for the Spirit to give us the wisdom and the insight to proclaim his word. We must learn to be at home in this mystery, remaining without control, clarity and certitude. We have only to acquiesce in mystery, and for the most part peacefully advance without seeing any way. Gradually, we experience that while we can do nothing of ourselves, we can nonetheless do all things in him who empowers us (*Ph* 4:13).

The solution to self-sufficiency and egocentricity is trust in God alone, honest abandonment to him in faith, hope, love. We need to remain carefree in God, casting our preoccupations upon him and directing only as his Spirit moves.

St. Therese of the Child Jesus describes her receptivity in spiritual direction this way:

"When it was given to me to penetrate into the sanctuary of souls, I saw immediately that the task was beyond my strength. Right away I threw myself like a little child into the arms of God and hid my face in his hair. I said: 'Lord, I am too little to nourish your children. But if you wish to use me to give each one something suitable, fill my little hand and without leaving your arms or turning my head I shall dispense your treasures to the souls who come to ask me for nourishment. If these souls find what I give them to their taste, I shall know that it is not of me. They owe it all to you. Furthermore, if these souls complain and find bitter what I impart, my peace will not be disturbed. I shall work to persuade them that this nourishment indeed comes from you, and I shall be careful not to seek any other for them.

"As soon as I understood that it was impossible for me to do anything by myself, the task no longer seemed difficult. I felt that the one thing necessary was for me to unite myself more and more to Jesus and 'everything else will be given to you as well' [*Lk* 12:31]. In fact, never has my hope been mistaken. God has seen fit to fill my little hand as often as it was necessary for nourishing the souls of my sisters. I admit that if I had depended in the least upon myself, I would very soon have had to give up."[2]

## C. Frustration

Spiritual directors who recognize their dependence on God do, nonetheless, question the value of this ministry in certain situations. We may feel that spiritual direction is a waste of time and energy. This is especially the case when the directee does not profit immediately from our guidance, or when we are so preoccupied with some other pressing project or responsibility that it becomes difficult to remain attentive to the directee. Such feelings of frustration may be especially intense when dealing with a directee who puts limits on how much truth s/he is willing to accept.

The endless repetition of the same difficulties and the same advice can at times make spiritual direction seem boring, monotonous and without challenge. Directors sometimes have, and impart, the impression that the whole exercise is meaningless. In reality, God-willed spiritual direction is always interiorly meaningful for both the directee and the director regardless of surface appearances.

Since spiritual direction pertains to the realm of spirit, its fruits are not readily apparent. We may be tempted to abandon this ministry altogether in order to do something which appears more useful: like teaching, writing, even more solitary prayer.

[2] *Therese*, pp. 237-238.

Because direction is so time and energy consuming, frequented directors have little time for anything else. The fact that spiritual direction is so exclusively one-to-one also poses certain problems. Other ministries ostensibly reach more people, and as a consequence we may feel that we are not touching a sufficient number of lives or achieving enough far-reaching results.

All these temptations arise from a quantitative perspective. In the world of quality, personal vocation and faith, no amount of quantitative analysis ever makes sense (1 *Co* 1:22-23; 27-28; 2:13).

All God asks is that we undergo our doubts, feelings and lack of challenge. Instead of feeling guilty about them or entertaining them, we should make every effort to remain wholeheartedly present to God within the directee. In a spirit of joy and generosity, we must transcend our feelings and function out of principle, out of a sense of responsibility and conviction. We should accept our ministry "as coming directly from God himself, and execute it with all zeal and attention as a work given by God and performed in his presence."[3]

These trials and frustrations are the spiritual exercises through which God deepens our own faith, hope and love. They are thus an effective instrument of transformation and purification in our personal spiritualization. Through them God challenges us as directors to greater spiritual maturity. God's challenge frequently consists in calling us to do our very best despite all apparent feelings to the contrary.

## D. Mistakes

Our poverty confronts us especially when we make mistakes in spiritual direction. For instance, in the course of discernment we do not perceive subtle or obvious signs of psychological, emotional or moral disorder. Besides not seeing, we may on occasion misread what we do see. It is not uncommon to interpret signs which in fact indicate a call to

[3]Theophan the Recluse, in *The Art of Prayer* (Faber, 1966) p. 240.

contemplative prayer as signs of spiritual backsliding, or in the context of vocational crisis to misinterpret negative signs for positive ones or vice versa.

Sooner or later one way or another, if we are conscientious, we become aware of our mistakes. Our first reaction is to feel that we have failed both God and the directee. We may question our competency and our gift. We may feel guilt and experience difficulty forgiving ourselves: How could I have been so blind? How could I have done such a thing?

Instead of wallowing in self-pity, self-blame or self-analysis, we have to humbly and maturely accept the fact that we have erred. We need to derive from the experience whatever we can learn. But God surely does not want us to go into a tailspin over our mistakes. We really are fallible. And God can convert our mistakes into good just as easily as he can any other difficulty (*Rm* 8:28).

Instead of dwelling on the past, we should start afresh from the present and strain forward. If there is something specific that we can do to correct the situation, naturally we must do it. But, when circumstances do not permit such a correction (e.g. when we are no longer in contact with the directee), we should let go all preoccupation with correction. We must believe that God will write straight with our crooked lines, and we must translate this faith into concrete behavior. All God asks is that we sincerely do our best to collaborate with the Spirit. Beyond that we leave all the rest to him.

Our mistakes arise from a variety of sources: closed-mindedness, prejudice for or against the directee, stubbornness, hesitancy to confront, predetermined ways and structures, rigidity, etc. Even being overly cautious about never making mistakes is itself a mistake. This hyper-caution focuses attention on our track record, rather than on God himself. Preoccupation over our mistakes is also a further mistake, since it emphasizes our supposed perfection rather than contentment with our poverty (2 *Co* 12:10).

Sometimes directors think that something is wrong with them because God in his wisdom chooses not to grant a particular insight. These directors react to such situations as if God *must* use *them* at all times and in all ways. God is perfectly free to bestow or to withhold any gift any time, for his own mysterious reasons. Furthermore, some directors believe that their ability to discern is directly related to the amount of time they spend in prayer and fasting. Surely we could all benefit by more in-depth prayer and self-discipline. But no one merits the grace of discernment. We cannot achieve it by any amount of personal effort. God gives it to and takes it away from whomever he pleases and for however long he wants.

Hindsight is a good teacher, but a poor judge. Sometimes, in retrospect we realize that a certain decision was a mistake, even though in reality it was as good a choice as we could make at the time. Discernment is ongoing. It is a dynamic process. Therefore, what is appropriate at one point may have to be discarded or modified later.

The greatest mistake is to persist in mistakes once they are recognized or to hold on to a lesser way once a better way is discerned.

## E. Vulnerability

A truly *spiritual* director is one who possesses a "heart of flesh" (*Ez* 36:26): that is, a heart which is open, loving, defenseless and sensitive. While vulnerability greatly facilitates our capacity to listen, it is also a source of much suffering. The more vulnerable we are, the more open we remain to be hurt time and time again.

Hurt may be occasioned by directees themselves. A person, for example, may turn us off because s/he does not like what is being said. Sometimes those for whom we pour out the most blood, sweat and tears respond with ingratitude, unjustified criticism or personal attack.

We may be hurt by others on account of the directee. For instance, the directee is a member of a community which is excessively structured and legalistic. Any growth of this person in freedom and responsibility will probably be interpreted by his/her religious superiors as arrogance, disobedience or individualism. The superior and/or community may then blame the director for ruining the directee's submissive disposition. The superior may go so far as to label the director incompetent, and try to prevent others from seeking his/her guidance. One occasionally hears political epitaphs like "liberal" or "communist" evoked in such contexts.

Usually, this type of behavior by directees or by those closely associated with them is not really a personal attack against the director. Rather, it is a defense mechanism. Trying desperately to maintain control of their previously secure world, these persons become threatened by the possibility of qualitative change. The director becomes the scapegoat in a particular issue, but the real problem lies elsewhere.

We need to appreciate this behavior for what it is. This understanding greatly assists us in absorbing the hurts as did Jesus: "Father, forgive them, for they know not what they do" (*Lk* 23:34). Without this appreciation we may be tempted to erect our own defense mechanisms. These can take the form of withdrawal from the directee, of thinking or speaking disparagingly of the opposing party, of becoming unduly negative or critical. The more gentle, loving and accepting we remain, the more we encourage the other to drop his/her defenses and begin communication.

## F. The Directee's Poverty

Not only do we as spiritual directors undergo our own personal poverty, but also we necessarily take upon ourselves something of the poverty of our directees. We undergo with our directees something of their struggle to become like Christ. Paul, reflecting on this aspect of his own spiritual parenthood, writes: "My children, I go through the pain of giving rebirth to you until Christ is formed in you" (*Ga* 4:19).

Seeing our directees writhe in their poverty, we can easily be tempted to try to remove their pain. Yet, to succumb to this temptation would indeed be unfortunate, since it would deprive them of a grace. We must let directees pass through their share of "groaning in the one great act of giving birth" (*Rm* 8:22). This passage is the only way for them to do their part in order to "fill up what is lacking in the sufferings of Christ" (*Col* 1:24). In this manner, they find their true identity in him.

Standing by helpless and without interfering while another person is agonizing can be heart-wrenching. There are times when like the prodigal father (*Lk* 15:11-13) we have to let directees go their own way even if we know they are probably heading for rock-bottom. All we can do in certain instances is to remain a supportive, silent presence to them in their struggles. We thus witness in a special way to the tender, merciful, infinitely long-suffering love of the Father.

Needless to say, we must have suitable outlets for our emotional upheavals at these times. If not, we become so preoccupied with the directee that we are unable to attend to anyone or anything else.

## G. Treasure in Earthenware Vessels

Through the experience of our poverty of spirit, God teaches us in no uncertain terms that the charism to awaken and quicken the life of the Spirit in the directee is truly *gift*: "We possess this treasure in earthenware vessels to make it clear that this overwhelming power is from God and not from us" (2 *Co* 4:7). Moreover, we appreciate like Jeremiah that "whenever the vessel that he is working on turns out wrong" as sometimes happens "he begins anew and works it into another vessel" (*Jr* 18:4). In poverty, we discover the unfathomable richness of God's wisdom (*Rm* 11:33-36). In weakness, we receive the strength of Christ (1 *Co* 1:25).

The making or breaking of spiritual directors depends often on their response to their own poverty. There are basically two choices: Either (1) we become eventually so disheartened and cynical that we refuse to become involved any further in spiritual direction. Or (2) in the realization that we cannot do it ourselves, we let God direct the directee his way. Thus, we let him use us or not use us precisely as he wills.

Dependent on God in our poverty, we begin to perceive this overwhelming power operative in and through the director-directee encounter. We experience in faith something of the transforming and purifying effect of God's love in each person. We grow in appreciation of our own call to be an instrument of the Spirit in the directee's spiritualization. Standing in awe before the mystery of Christ being formed in the directee and in ourselves, we experience that God's power is truly at its best in weakness (2 *Co* 12:9).

*Chapter 14*

# Personalized Retreats

The term "retreat" designates a time during which a person, either individually or as a member of a group, goes apart from the usual occupations and routines of living in order to celebrate the life that lies within them. The amount of time spent in retreat may be brief or prolonged.

Most retreats fall under one of the following four broad descriptions:

(1) *The preached retreat.* This is what most people understand by retreat. A number of persons come together and are given several conferences a day on some aspect of spirituality. Outside the conferences the participants pray, do meditative reading, share together in faith and in some cases even socialize with each other. Silence may or may not be emphasized, depending on the retreat director and the desire of the group. Those drawn to this type of retreat are not usually seeking personal guidance. When the group is large it may be impossible for the retreat director to provide individual spiritual direction except for those few who expressly request it.

(2) *The directed retreat.* A person goes off to be alone and pray in silence and solitude. The retreatant chooses or is appointed a director. They meet usually once a day to

discuss whatever needs attention. There are innumerable formats which a directed retreat can take. One of the most popular is the Ignatian Exercises, whether for a week or for thirty days. Because of the one-to-one dimension of a directed retreat, the director can adapt to the specific needs of the retreatant. Unfortunately, not all directors are in fact so adaptable.

(3) *The personalized retreat.* This retreat is entirely tailored to the personal needs of the retreatant. The retreatant does not fit into any prearranged plan or sequence. The retreatant is taken as a unique individual so much so that the whole format of the retreat evolves spontaneously out of his/her needs. The director helps to identify and interpret these needs.

The personalized retreat differs from the directed retreat mentioned above not only by its intensified accent on spontaneity and individualization, but also with regard to the basic stance of the director. In a directed retreat, the retreatant usually relies on the director for input. The director really does direct the retreat, and generally spends a lot of time with the retreatant. In a personalized retreat, the director primarily listens. Virtually all input is received from the Spirit, from within the retreatant. Thus, the director need not spend so much time with the retreatant. A "word" here or there usually suffices.

The directed retreat is generally best suited for a person beginning or advanced in discursive prayer. The personalized retreat, on the other hand, is especially helpful for a person being drawn to contemplation.[1]

One may also speak of a personalized directed retreat wherein the basic thrusts of both are intermingled. This form is appropriate for the person teetering at the threshold of contemplative prayer.

A particularly effective variation of the personalized retreat is one in a communal setting. That is, a group of persons come together who each want to make a personalized retreat under the guidance of a spiritual director.

[1]See *Contemplation*, pp. 53-84.

Usually such a group is small in number. This allows the director sufficient leisure to provide in-depth direction to each person. In addition to individualized guidance, the director may offer group spiritual direction. This can occur through the Eucharistic homily and in a brief daily conference on some aspect of interior growth. Some provision may also be made for occasional faith sharing on a communal basis. For instance, the group can come together in the evening for optional shared reflection on a designated scriptural passage. Although these limited activities are incorporated into the silence and solitude of the retreat, the principal thrust remains on personal encounter with God.

Even a large group retreat can be personalized and directed in this manner if a sufficient number of spiritual directors are available for individual guidance.

(4) *The private retreat.* A person goes off to some secluded place to be entirely alone and pray. S/he enters into intense silence and solitude. By definition, this form of retreat does not have a regular human director, although the retreatant may avail of one on specific occasions (e.g. to celebrate the sacrament of reconciliation). God himself remains the immediate director of a private retreat.

Generally, this retreatant does not participate directly in any group activity other than the daily celebration of the Eucharist and possibly meals. Being alone in order to pray, however, does not necessarily mean complete physical absence of other people. In the midst of others, a person can maintain profound interior silence and solitude. Thus, it is not uncommon to discover certain retreatants within a group on a preached retreat who are in effect making a private retreat.

Normal growth in prayer corresponds to these four broad descriptions of retreats. At the outset of a deepening prayer life, vocal and communal prayer are especially meaningful. Hence, one may be drawn to the preached retreat. Usually, a prolonged period of discursive meditation follows this initial phase of prayer development. The directed retreat is quite helpful during this meditative stage. Once God begins to lead the person into contemplative prayer, the personalized retreat is specifically appropriate. The private retreat is wholly open-ended, and is best suited for the person whom God has directed into full-blown contemplation.

The theology and ministry of preached, directed and private retreats are generally well-known. For the remainder of this chapter we concentrate on the personalized retreat.

## A. Principles Governing Personalized Retreats

Integral to personalized retreats are these seven principles: (1) These retreats partake of a desert experience. (2) They take place in a milieu of silence and solitude. (3) A person is drawn by God to make this kind of retreat. (4) The retreat is scripturally based. (5) It is personalized. (6) Its thrust is towards freedom of spirit. (7) The retreatant receives some guidance from a spiritual director.

### (1) THE DESERT EXPERIENCE

The theology of personalized retreats has its origin in the biblical concept of desert.

The prototype of the desert experience is the exodus. God led his people out of Egyptian slavery not only into the desert but also through the desert. Throughout their journey, the Israelites were continuously caught up in the struggle between a sincere desire to surrender themselves to Yahweh and an innate resistance against him. While God was pressing them forward towards freedom, the Hebrews were constantly straining backwards, longing for the relatively complacent existence of Egypt.

Having been freed from physical bondage, the Israelites experienced in the desert the full impact of their interior slavery: their egocentrism. "In the desert, when God began giving them the heavenly food which contains in itself all delight ... they continued to crave for the tasty meat and onions they had eaten in Egypt. Their palates were attracted to these rather than to the delicate sweetness of the angelic manna. So they wept and grieved for fleshmeat in the midst of this heavenly food."[2]

Centuries later the Hebrews looked back on their desert sojourn as an ideal time in their salvation history. They saw how, in their absolute dependence on God and despite their resistance and sin, Yahweh had lavished upon them his merciful love and had provided for their every need.

The earthly sojourn of Jesus is the example par excellence of the desert experience: "He emptied himself, taking on the form of a servant.... He humbled himself becoming obedient unto death, death on a cross. Therefore, God exalted him" (*Ph* 2:7-9).

The desert evokes aloneness, starkness, vast horizons, mystery, silence, timelessness, subtle life, gentle breezes, violent storms, cool nights, blistering heat, magnificent sunsets, blinding light. The desert demands communion with nature, communion with one's deepest self, and above all communion with the Father. In a word, the desert is solitude. All these experiences were integral to Jesus's interior life: "He would always go off to some deserted place and pray" (*Lk* 5:16). After the cure of Simon Peter's mother-in-law, long before dawn, "Jesus arose, left the house and went off to a solitary spot to pray" (*Mk* 1:35). "Full of the Holy Spirit, Jesus returned from the Jordan and was led by the Spirit through the desert" (*Lk* 4:1).

Jesus taught his disciples to do likewise: "You must come away to some desert place all by yourselves and rest awhile" (*Mk* 6:31).

The desert is more than just a solitary *place.* It is primarily a reality of the heart. In the desert, God opens us to his transforming and consuming love. Desert symbolizes the ongoing, interior process of dying to self in order to rise in Christ. The interior desert produces its effect whether we are in exterior solitude or in the midst of feverish activity. In

---

[2]*Night,* I, 9, 5.

making a personalized retreat, retreatants enter into an intensely explicit phase of their ongoing desert experience. They each undergo their desert before, during and after the retreat proper.

The desire to make a personalized retreat may be quickened by any number of factors. Perhaps a retreatant feels a need to reestablish priorities or to better integrate ministry, community or family life into his/her relationship with God. The retreatant may be undergoing a crisis in faith, prayer or vocation.

Frequently, however, a person seeks to make a personalized retreat not because of any particular crisis or difficulty at all. Rather, the person yearns to take the leisure to enter more intimately into loving communion with God. The retreatant is well aware that this communion is operative in every aspect of life, but s/he needs to give this divine intimacy space and time to be and to become more intense.


## (2) SILENCE AND SOLITUDE

The emphasis in a personalized retreat is on interiority: "The Word, the Son of God, together with the Father and the Holy Spirit, is hidden in essence and in presence in the intimate being of the soul. Therefore, the soul who wants to find him must be detached from all things and enter within itself in deepest recollection."[3]

God dwells not only within us, but also within every creature outside us. Yet, before we can perceive him outside, we must first discover him within ourselves. "I did not find you outside, Lord, because I wrongly sought you there, you who were within."[4] Thus, to find the real God we must enter deep within ourselves so that passing on through and beyond ourselves we may encounter him who dwells within us in mystery.

---

[3]*Canticle*, 1, 6. See *Receptivity*, pp. 18-23, 41-49, 114-120.

[4]Pseudo-Augustine, *Soliloquies of the Soul to God*, 1, 31 (*PL:* 40:888).

This language of being drawn into solitude, of entering into ourselves is metaphoric. It refers to direct, interpersonal communion between God and the soul. This communion is exclusive in the sense that the whole focus of our deepest being is entirely on God. Yet, it is also all-inclusive, since in this loving interchange everyone and everything are attained in and through God. The analogy of entering — whether into solitude or into ourselves — is particularly apt for the personalized retreat, since it stresses the interiority of this communion to which Jesus invites us: "Remain in me, as I remain in you" (*Jn* 15:4). Thus, we enter most deeply into ourselves when we are most detached from ourselves and from every creature. Self is neither the focus of this communion, nor its locus. Our self is that which is transformed in God.

The starting point of a personalized retreat is personal experience of the indwelling Trinity: "Do you acknowledge that Jesus Christ is really within you?" (2 *Co* 13:5). In solitude of heart, each of us plumbs these depths in which "I live now, no longer I, but Christ lives in me." (*Ga* 2:20). In solitude, we encounter by faith the mystery of God abiding within us as well as the mystery of our own life "hidden with Christ in God" (*Col* 3:3).

In personalized retreats, two essential aids assist the retreatant to enter more deeply into this solitude of heart. They are *silence* and *exterior solitude.*

Silence is far more than the absence of talking. Silence, in essence, is listening. There is always something going on within the human spirit. It is never totally blank or static. If we are not doing, we are receiving. If we are not chattering, we are listening. This is true exteriorly. It is especially true interiorly.

Silence is also a condition necessary in order to listen more deeply. And it is a precondition for speaking or responding with wisdom. We receive what we are to say. The authentic word emerges out of silence. "The Father spoke but one Word, who was his Son. This Word he speaks forever in eternal silence. And in silence, it must be listened to by the soul."[5] Silence then is truly a way of being with God and of being with one another in him.

Exterior solitude is likewise far more than being physically alone. It is being alone in order to be more immediately with God. Furthermore, in being alone with God, we soon discover the mysterious bond by which we are united with all creation: for "in him, we all live and move and are" (*Ac* 17:28).

Neither silence nor exterior solitude are ends in themselves. They are means by which we seek to deepen our communion with God and with others in him.

Why are silence and solitude so important? Seeking them out is a positive gesture expressing our willingness to let go our props, our crutches, our defenses. In silence and solitude we increasingly let go the diversions which we use to hide from the truth of ourselves and of God.

These activity-oriented attachments divert us and turn us away from the one-thing-necessary (*Lk* 10:42) which can help us begin our ascent to truth. "That one thing is the sense of our own emptiness, our poverty, our limitations, and of the inability of created things to satisfy our profound need for reality and for truth."[6]

In the context of a personalized retreat, retreatants not only let go their diversions, but also they are freed from their usual God-given responsibilities. Thus, they remain alone for a time loving their Beloved. This is how they celebrate par excellence the life which underlies these responsibilities.

In silence and solitude, free from normal preoccupations and duties, the retreatant abides in God as a child in the arms of its father. The person enters voluntarily into the truth of his/her inner poverty, emptiness, limitations. Therein s/he experiences the infinite love of God. In short, in silence and solitude the retreatant enters in an unparalleled manner into *nada* so as to discover *todo*.

---

[5]St. John of the Cross, *Dichos de luz y amor, BAC* 5th. ed., #99.

[6]Thomas Merton, *The Ascent to Truth* (Harcourt, 1951) p. 25. See *Receptivity*, pp. 18-21.

## (3) DRAWN BY GOD

Our thirst for silence and solitude is not something of our own making. Seeking out silence and solitude is in reality a response to God's personal invitation: "I, Yahweh, will lure her into the desert. There I will commune with her heart" (*Ho* 2:16).

Personalized retreats are not for everyone anytime. A person must be drawn by God to make one. No one with any sense wanders aimlessly into a desert: physical or otherwise. Personalized retreats are not fads. They are not spiritual status symbols. They are not even the thing to do. They are never "in." In the right measure and at the right time God himself awakens a person to an inexplicable need for the desert, for some real silence and solitude. He may then draw that individual to make a personalized retreat.

## (4) SCRIPTURALLY BASED

Our spiritual food for the journey through the desert (1 *K* 19:7; *Is* 55:1-3) is the word of God, especially as revealed in scripture. Through listening to this word, the Spirit opens us to receive more directly Christ, the Word incarnate.

Directed retreats are also scripturally based. But the approach to scripture is normally quite different in the personalized retreat as compared with the directed retreat.

Since the context of the directed retreat is discursive, the discursive pondering of entire passages is stressed. The retreatant works the passage over, as it were, gleaning actively from it all the insight and practical application possible. The retreatant meditates, in the full sense of the term, on the scriptures.

In a personalized retreat, on the other hand, the retreatant listens to God through the scriptures. Instead of working them over, the retreatant remains affectively receptive before them and lovingly attentive to God beyond them. Thus, the retreatant lets the word of God work him/her over, if God wills. In this context, a line or even a single word of scripture more than suffices. The retreatant contemplates, in the strict sense of the term, the God of scripture.[7]

## (5) PERSONALIZED

In both the Old and the New Testaments, God is revealed as infinitely personal: as the God of love. "If Yahweh set his heart on you and chose you, it was not because you were the greatest of peoples....It was simply for love of you" (*Dt* 7:7-8). "Thus says Yahweh, 'You are precious in my eyes. You are honored, and I love you'" (*Is* 43:1, 4). "Yahweh says this, 'I have loved you with an everlasting love. I am constant in my love for you'" (*Jr* 31:3). "God so loved the world that he gave his only begotten Son" (*Jn* 3:16). "God is love" (1 *Jn* 4:8, 16). "Having loved his own in the world, he loved them to the end" (*Jn* 13:1).

God's love for each of us is personal and intimate. As such, the transforming and purifying influence of his love is completely tailored to our individual personalities, life circumstances, strengths and weaknesses. Every one of us is called to render a unique gift of self to God. Because we are first loved by him, we can love God in return, and we contribute to the building up of his kingdom in a manner so unique that no other person can duplicate or replace our contribution.

A personalized retreat is entirely geared towards allowing the retreatant to make a uniquely personal response to God. This retreat is grounded in the utmost respect for the mystery of each individual being created "in the image and likeness of God" (*Gn* 1:26). Every person is recognized as a singular expression of the Word becoming flesh and of flesh becoming transformed in the Word.

The personalized retreat is a means of drawing the retreatant beyond the surface of daily existence to plumb the depths of his/her loving union with God. This retreat discourages the retreatant from routinely going through

---

[7]See *Contemplation*, pp. 36-43.

endless rounds of devotional practices and adopting meaningless methods of prayer. The personalized retreat should
facilitate the retreatant's openness and receptivity to the
indwelling Father, Son and Spirit.

Moreover this retreat is personalized in that retreatants
come at a particular point in the process of their spiritualization. The director does not impose any expectations or
assumptions. The director accepts retreatants as they are,
wherever they are on their journey to the Father

Acceptance, however, is not to be confused with complacent indulgence or laxity. This latter lets retreatants be, but
"be" in the sense of allowing them to wallow in their egocentrism without any call to transcendence. True acceptance,
on the other hand, acknowledges who a person is and where
a person is. Acceptance uses these facts as the basis of
challenge to greater spiritualization. Acceptance is the starting point for building upon the grace that a retreatant has
already received.

The specific way of personalizing a retreat emerges from
listening to God within the retreatant. Through the manifestation of heart, the Spirit gives the director indications of
what is appropriate with regard to the details of the retreat.
These particulars include: which scriptural passages and
other spiritual reading (if any) to suggest, the number of
hours of solitary prayer per day to be recommended, the
frequency and length of meetings between the director and
the retreatant.

## (6) FREEDOM OF SPIRIT

Beyond a minimum horarium necessary for smooth communal functioning (for example, a specific time for Eucharistic celebrations, meals and meetings with the spiritual
director), retreatants are free from exterior structure and
schedules. In a personalized retreat retreatants do not have
to fit into a fixed method of prayer. No one regiments their
every movement.

While there is no imposed structure or predetermined
schedule, a concrete, practical daily schedule does emerge as

the retreatant listens to God. Having discerned with the director what the Spirit seems to be indicating with regard to use of time, the retreatant knows intuitively from one day to the next when and how to schedule solitary prayer, reading, recreation, etc.

It is not important that a person do everything at exactly the same time each day throughout the retreat. However, perseverence in whatever the Spirit is indicating is extremely important. Discipline is an integral aspect of true freedom.

The exterior freedom which characterizes the personalized retreat disposes the retreatant to receive more abundantly the interior freedom and discipline of the Spirit. The retreatant thus becomes increasingly capable of living according to the law of the Spirit of life which is setting him/her free from the law of sin and death (*Rm* 8:2).

## (7) DIRECTED

In a personalized retreat, God calls the retreatant to share with a director something of what is transpiring in the silence and solitude.

Spiritual direction is an important safeguard in the context of personalized retreats. Listening to God with the director, the retreatant tests the authenticity of interior movements. Guidance ensures that the person is truly searching for God, not merely drifting. Its challenge keeps the retreatant from narcissistically following his/her own whims and fancies.

Spiritual direction helps the retreatant sift out truth from illusion, reality from fantasy, self from God. It helps dispel imaginary difficulties. It assists the person in working maturely through the obstacles that genuinely exist. Furthermore, in direction the retreatant receives the positive advice and encouragement which facilitate a forward thrust towards the Spirit.

At the outset of the personalized retreat, the retreatant normally gives the director an overview of his/her present spiritual life. This consists in a general description of ministry, family or community life, prayer habits and any areas of immediate difficulty. This overview provides valuable input regarding the personalization of the retreat.

The director and the retreatant explore together the latter's expectations pertaining to the retreat. Jesus himself challenged people to examine their reasons for seeking the desert: "What did you go out into the desert to see?" (*Lk* 7:24-27). He questioned them on three areas of misguided motivations and expectations:

"A reed swaying in the breeze?" That is: Have you drifted aimlessly into the desert? Are you a curiosity seeker? Do you want merely to see what it is like? Is your desire for solitude a fickle whim or fancy? Did you come into the desert because other people seem to be doing it?

"No? Then what did you go out to see? A man dressed in fine clothes?" Are you seeking solitude for the sake of pleasure, rest, vacation? Are you looking for a good time? Is your desire to be alone your way of escaping your responsibilities or withdrawing from the tensions and conflicts of your life?

"Well, then what did you go out to see? A prophet?" Did you come to the desert seeking a palpable experience of God? Are you looking for something (or someone) spectacular and moving? Do you want to be pampered or consoled? Are you seeking a sort of honeymoon with the Lord which is completely divorced from the reality of your life?

"Yes, I tell you, you will find much more than a prophet." You will encounter God himself in the desert. You will encounter Father, Son and Spirit in faith and in mystery, in darkness and in night, in hope and in love.

Needless to say, God can use misguided motives and expectations to bring about his purposes. But it behooves the retreatant, nonetheless, to explore his/her motives, be they mature or immature. Frequently, persons discover that their reasons for initially going into the desert are not exactly the reasons that God has in drawing them there.

From the outset, the director helps the retreatant focus on the core of the retreat, which is to remain loving God and to remain being loved by him every moment of each day. Whether or not something appears to be happening, the retreatant must be content to persevere in listening, in waiting upon God.

When a person begins the retreat with a particular problem or at a time of personal crisis, it is especially crucial that God remain the central focus. In this instance, the retreatant can so easily make the problem itself the center of attention, thereby spending much time and energy probing and analyzing it in an effort to find a facile solution. Going this route, the person ends up usually more frustrated and confused than before.

The director should encourage such a person to remain in loving attentiveness to God. The retreatant should not try directly either to analyze or not to analyze the difficulty. S/he needs to keep lovingly attentive to God and maintain an open mind and heart. Thus, the retreatant will be ready to receive whatever the Spirit wills. What is to come forth into consciousness emerges at God's pace. As the Spirit gradually sheds light on the difficulty, the retreatant can then leisurely ponder and search into the issue in question. "Set your heart on God and everything else will be given to you as well" (*Lk* 12:31).

## B. General Approaches to Conducting Personalized Retreats

There are at least two general avenues which a director may follow in conducting personalized retreats. Some retreatants are naturally more spontaneous. These want a freer hand in letting their retreat unfold. Others are naturally more structured. These are most at home when the director makes specific suggestions regarding the construct of their retreat.

The determining factor indicating which approach to follow is the suitability of a given approach for the retreatant's interior life. This information is obtained quite simply by posing these two questions to the retreatant: (1) What has your prayer life consisted in concretely over the past six months to a year? And (2) do you have any particular

preferences regarding the format of this retreat? The retreatant's response to these two questions furnishes the director
with ample criteria for discerning the appropriate approach.

## (1) APPROACH FOR A MORE SPONTANEOUS RETREATANT

Virtually everyone wants and needs some spiritual input
during a retreat. In a personalized retreat the prime source
of this input is the scriptures, whether Old or New
Testament.

For the more spontaneous retreatant, the director might
give advice to this effect:

Choose any book of scripture: be it a gospel account, an
epistle, the book of Psalms, whatever. Approach this book
with the attitude of Samuel: "Here I am, Lord, your listening servant" (1 *Sm* 3:10).

Most of the time when we approach scripture we have
some practical purpose in mind. We are preparing a talk,
looking for some insight, guiding people's lives (2 *Tm* 3:16).
All of which is fitting in its proper place. But in the context
of a personalized retreat, leave aside all such intentions and
just *listen* to the word of God. Instead of trying to get
something out of it, let it evoke in you whatever God wills.
Do not belabor God's word. Remain receptive before it.

To choose a book of scripture in these circumstances does
not require an elaborate process of discernment. Go with
your intuition. Perhaps for some time you have been drawn
to Jeremiah or John. Listen to God now in one of them.

Listening is distinct from hearing. We hear sounds. We
hear noises. We hear voices. But we listen to some-one.
Listening denotes affective communion between persons.
When we listen to the scriptures we commune with our
loving Father in them, beyond them. If we listen deeply
enough and lovingly enough, we do not necessarily hear
anything at all. Listening in this deeper sense is the quintessence of contemplation.[8]

[8]See *Contemplation*, pp. 32-33, 36-43, 141-147.

"Here I am, Lord, your listening servant." "Here I am" means just that. You are there: no tricks, no gimmicks, no baggage. You are there: poor, simple, humble before God receiving whatever he wants you to receive at that moment. You have no expectations, no demands, not even any specific desires. There is just you in him and he in you.

Begin with verse 1, chapter 1 of the book that God has moved you to choose. Read it slowly, leisurely, receptively. Pick it up at will. Put it down at will. Spend as much time as you want on any given passage, sentence or word. It is not necessary to finish the book by the end of the retreat.

If the book is long, you may wish to single out only a portion: for example, Matthew's sermon on the mount or the servant hymns in deutero-Isaiah. None of that makes any difference as long as you are drawn to the book or passages, and listen.

This manner of approaching scripture accentuates the spontaneity of a contemplatively inclined retreatant. It affords the person greater freedom to be directed by God. It also frees the director from much concentration on trying to figure out what to suggest next to the retreatant. Thus, the director remains more receptive than active in listening to God within the retreatant.

On occasion, it may be appropriate for the director to suggest a particular book or passage of scripture. The director and the retreatant may wish to discuss and discern together which specific readings to choose. But usually it is better to give the person carte blanche and see what happens. In the context of a personalized retreat, it is always better to begin with maximum freedom, and only later if the retreatant cannot handle it responsibly to introduce structure as needed.

While scripture remains the *prime* source of spiritual input during this retreat, it is not necessarily the only source. The director may see fit to suggest some other reading. The retreatant may also have a particular author or book to which s/he is inclined. This can be appropriate, provided that the retreat does not turn into a study session. One's faith experience during a personalized retreat may quite legitimately need to seek some understanding. But prayer, not study, is the proper focus of personalized retreats.

At times and with certain passages, the retreatant may receive considerable enlightenment. At other times and with other passages: *nada*, pure aridity. This may even occur with texts which have been favorites in the past. In reality, none of this matters at all. If a certain passage moves a person deeply, fine. S/he should receive all that the passage has to impart. If another passage says nothing at all, that can be fine too. The retreatant is still there humbly listening to God. S/he must receive *nada* with the same equanimity as *todo*.

Needless to say, this meditative reading should be performed apart from the time designated for solitary prayer. For persons who are in the habit of taking regularly an hour or so daily for contemplative prayer, four or five prayer periods per day during the retreat are generally advisable. Because such persons frequently go well over an hour in their prayer periods, it is important to give them some leeway. But no one should be encouraged to go under an hour, unless of course some unexpected exterior circumstance occurs (e.g., one is praying outdoors, and it begins to rain). For a person who prays in solitude for brief periods fairly regularly, three or four one hour periods daily are usually recommended. The director does not want to overburden the retreatant with prayer periods. If a climate of sufficient leisure is created, the retreatant will spontaneously pray more.

How is the retreatant to approach these periods of solitary prayer? In a word: contemplatively. That is, the director is to encourage the retreatant to wait upon God in loving attentiveness in the attitude of Moses (*Ex* 3:4), Samuel (1 *Sm* 3:10), Isaiah (*Is* 6:9), Mary (*Lk* 1:38): Here I am, Lord, your listening servant.

If something is needed to begin the prayer period, the retreatant may choose a verse, a phrase or a word that stood out in meditative reading. But this should be limited to a brief text for a given prayer period. Otherwise the hour will be spent looking for one passage after another, rather than in prayer with God.

At all times, the soul prays as it *can* — as it is spontaneously and intuitively moved at a given moment — and not as it thinks or assumes it *should.*[9]

## (2) APPROACH FOR A MORE STRUCTURED RETREATANT

This approach is based upon the spirit of the previous one, but presupposes that the retreatant either cannot handle or does not want quite so much freedom in planning the retreat. Thus, the retreatant asks the director for specific suggestions and a basic structure, or the director sees the need for this without being asked. The following are some concrete suggestions of our own which have proven helpful.

The director conducts the retreat in such a way that each day centers around a theme chosen to meet the spiritual needs of the retreatant. Besides assigning specific biblical passages on the theme of the day for each period of solitary prayer, the director may also assign other appropriate material for meditative reflection.

For example, a person wants to make a retreat of six full days. Both the director and the retreatant discern that five hours of solitary prayer daily are appropriate.

After the retreatant has calmed down and settled in, the director may suggest on the evening prior to the first day an hour of prayer focusing on the theme of "Christ in me" using either 2 *Co* 13:5-6 or *Ga* 2:19-20. The next six days could be spent on the following themes:

| | |
|---|---|
| *Day 1 (Creation)* | *Gn* 1:27, 31; 1 *Co* 7:29-31; *Rm* 8:22-25; *Col* 1:15-17; *Jn* 3:16-17. |
| *Day 2 (Call)* | *Dt* 7:6-9; 1 *Sm* 3:10; 1 *Tm* 1:12-13; 1 *Co* 1:26-27; *Jn* 21:18-19. |

[9]See *Contemplation*, pp. 53-59.

*Day 3 (Conversion)*    *Jr* 31:3, 33 or *Ez* 36:24-28; *Jl* 2:12-13; 2 *Co* 12: 7-10; *Rm* 8:28-29; *Mk* 1:15.

*Day 4 (Cross)*    *Jb* 5:17-18; *Lk* 9:23; 1 *Co* 1:18, 23-25; *Col* 1:20, 24; *Lk* 24:25-26.

*Day 5 (Prayer)*    *Dt* 4:7, 29; *Rm* 8:26-27; *Lk* 1:38; *Mk* 1:35; *Lk* 22:41-44.

*Day 6 (Spirit)*    *Rm* 7:14-25; *Rm* 8:5-6; *Rm* 8:14-17; 1 *Co* 2:10, 13, 15; *Jn* 14:26.

On the morning following the last full day, the retreatant might focus on the theme of recapitulation of all in Christ using 1 *Co* 15:28, *Col* 2:9 or *Eph* 3:14-21.

Regardless of the approach used in a personalized retreat, the director and the retreatant together determine the frequency and the length of time necessary for their meetings. In a week long retreat, it is generally necessary to meet daily for about half an hour. Should the retreat be more prolonged — thirty or forty days — meetings every other day for fifteen or twenty minute periods usually suffice.

In making a personalized retreat, the retreatant should take some time each day for recreation: jogging, a stroll in the woods, some light reading, etc. However, when the retreat is prolonged, the retreatant should also take a block of time (several hours at a stretch) per week for personal leisure. This time away from the usual intensity of the retreat helps the person become physically and psychologically recreated for whatever lies ahead.

The director may also encourage the retreatant to engage in an hour or so of manual work each day. Manual labor not only meets certain needs of the person trying to work off tension and frustration, but also it contributes to building community in Christ.

Should a retreatant desire more solitude and silence than usual (e.g., by going to a hermitage), s/he should discern the authenticity of this desire with the director. There are otherwise sincere persons who in effect look upon a hermitage experience as the thing to do, a fad, a spiritual status symbol.

Since resolutions pertain more to discursive prayer than to contemplation, they are not especially appropriate at the conclusion of a personalized retreat. However, the retreatant may spontaneously wish to recapitulate the gist of the faith experience. The director should encourage this recapitulation. It may take the form of choosing a single scriptural passage (one verse or less) which epitomizes the particular significance of the retreat for the retreatant.

# Conclusion

Throughout this study we have brought theological and pastoral reflection to bear on the mystery and charism of spiritual direction. Like every mystery, we know better what it is not than what it is.

Some receive this gift-freely-given to a greater degree than others do. For some, spiritual direction is a full-time ministry. For others, they exercise this charism only once or twice in a lifetime. All do not experience this gift in the same way. Indeed, the more contemplatively inclined both the director and the directee become, the more necessarily unique and spontaneous is the direction which God indicates.

One cannot prepare for the ministry or practice of spiritual direction the way a med-student prepares to be a surgeon or a defense lawyer prepares a case. Serious study, perseverance in prayer and honest self-discipline are required for any vibrant interior life. These same qualities are also the matrix out of which God calls forth competent spiritual direction. These qualities, furthermore, help discern the possible presence of this charism as well as aid the director's collaboration with the Spirit in refining this gift.

There is no such thing as a ninety-day wonder (much less a two-week wonder!) in spiritual direction. No one becomes a director after a crash course, regardless how one's certificate may read. Spiritual direction is pure gift, both for the director as well as for the directee. And consequently, so is their relationship. This gift is fragile. It is delicate. It needs to grow, mature, expand and intensify. It is to be treated as a grace from God himself. Therefore, "I beseech you to walk worthily in the vocation to which you are called" (*Eph* 4:1).

Spiritual direction in the deepest sense — in the sense that we have been developing throughout this book — is distinct from counseling, from opening up to a confidant and from sharing with a close friend. Spiritual direction is distinguishable from counseling in that the latter is client-oriented and deals primarily with the observable and behavioral aspects of the human person. Spiritual direction remains first, foremost and always God-oriented: listening to him and to his mysterious, ineffable ways within the directee. Spiritual direction transcends opening up to a confidant in that the latter usually presupposes a lengthy acquaintance: someone who has seen the other through many up's and down's. One's spiritual director may also be a confidant of sorts, but spiritual direction itself is generally more regular and much more profound than one's up's and down's. Rarely is a spiritual director an intimate friend with a directee. Indeed, a given person seldom has more than three or four really close friends during an entire lifetime. Intimate friendship requires mutual, personal sharing on all levels of human interrelatedness: social, intellectual, emotional as well as spiritual. Obviously, close friendship is a considerably more all-embracing relationship than director-directee, and it implies a very different rapport of one with the other. We all need an intimate friend or two. Most of us can be helped immensely by a real confidant. Many benefit from counseling or therapy at certain crucial periods. Some are blessed with spiritual directors whether for a lifetime or for a brief time. In every case, God himself provides for each one of us, guiding us in his way.

Eternal life in God is the goal of spiritual direction. But within that universal goal there are certain more immediate goals: (1) The director must decrease, so that Christ may increase (*Jn* 3:30). (2) The directee has to become progressively emancipated. The directee grows more and more capable of discerning the indwelling Father, Son and Spirit without the aid of a human director. (3) The directee thus becomes increasingly aware of all the other ways through which God reveals spiritual direction.

Paradoxically, therefore, spiritual direction leads to spiritual non-direction, because it is only in losing our way that we truly begin to find The Way: "The one who loses his/her life for my sake will find it" (*Mt* 10:39).

*Sic finis libri*
*non autem operis*
*nequaquam mysterii.*

"Let us now go forward on the same road that has brought us where we are..." (*Ph* 3:16).

# Select Bibliography

## BOOKS

Baker, Augustine. *Holy Wisdom.* Burns and Oates, 1972.

English, John. *Choosing Life.* Paulist, 1978.

Francis de Sales. *Introduction to the Devout Life,* 1, 4.

Gabriel of St. Mary Magdalen. *The Spiritual Director: According to the Principles of St. John of the Cross.* Mercier, 1951.

Gratton, Carolyn. *Guidelines for Spiritual Direction.* Dimension, 1980.

de Guilbert, Joseph. *The Theology of the Spiritual Life.* Sheed and Ward, 1953, pp. 155-186.

Haughey, John. *The Conspiracy of God: The Holy Spirit in Men.* Doubleday, 1973.

John of the Cross. *Living Flame of Love,* 3, 27-62.

John of the Cross. *The Ascent of Mount Carmel,* II, 26, 11-18.

Laplace, Jean. *Preparing for Spiritual Direction.* Franciscan Herald, 1975.

Leech, Kenneth. *Soul Friend.* Harper and Row, 1977.

McNeill, John. *A History of the Cure of Souls.* Harper Torchbooks, 1965.

Merton, Thomas. *Spiritual Direction and Meditation.* Liturgical, 1960.

Merton, Thomas. "The Spiritual Father in the Desert Tradition," in *Contemplation in a World of Action*. Image, 1973.

Nemeck, Francis Kelly and Coombs, Marie Theresa. *Contemplation*. Michael Glazier, 1982.

Neufelder, Jerome and Coelho, Mary, eds. *Writings on Spiritual Direction by Great Christian Mystics*. Seabury, 1982.

Parente, Pascal. *Spiritual Direction*. St. Paul, 1961.

Richards, Innocentia, trans. *Discernment of Spirits*. Liturgical Press, 1970.

Sackett, Frederick. *The Spiritual Director in an Ecclesiastical Seminary*. University of Ottawa Press, 1945.

Sommerfeldt, John, ed. *Abba*. Cistercian Studies, n. 38, Cistercian Publications, 1982.

Sullivan, John, ed. *Spiritual Direction*. ICS Publications, 1980, pp. 3-100.

Teresa of Jesus. *Life*, esp. chs. 5, 13, 28, 30.

Teresa of Jesus. *Way of Perfection*. Ch. 4 and appendix to ch. 4 in E. Allison Peers, trans. Sheed and Ward, 1950.

Theresa of the Child Jesus. *Story of a Soul: The Autobiography of St. Therese of Lisieux*. ICS Publications, 1975, pp. 239-242.

Van Kaam, Adrian. *The Dynamics of Spiritual Self Direction*. Dimension, 1976.

_____ "Direction spirituelle," *Dictionnaire de spiritualité*. 20-23, 1002-1291.

## LETTERS/WRITINGS OF SPIRITUAL DIRECTORS

Bossuet, Jacques. *Letters of Spiritual Direction.* Morehouse-Gorham, 1958.

de Caussade, Jean-Pierre. *Abandonment to Divine Providence.* Herder, 1921.

Fénelon, Francis. *Letters to Men and Women.* Newman, 1957.

Fénelon, Francis. *The Spiritual Letters.* St.Anselm, 1893.

Fénelon, Francis. *Letters of Love and Counsel.* Harcourt, 1964.

Francis de Sales. *Letters to Persons in Religion.* Newman, 1943.

Francis de Sales. *Selected Letters.* Faber, 1960.

John of the Cross. *Letters* in Peers, vol. 3, pp. 237-278 or Kavanaugh and Rodriguez, pp. 685-706.

Macarius. *Russian Letters of Direction: 1834-1860.* St. Vladimir, 1975.

Merton, Thomas, trans. *The Wisdom of the Desert.* New Direction, 1960.

Ward, Benedicta, trans. *The Sayings of the Desert Fathers.* Cistercian Publications, 1975.

_____ *A Pistle of Discrecioun of Stirings* in *Contemplative Review,* 10 (1, 1977) 9-19 or in Wolters, Clifton, trans. *A Study of Wisdom: Three Tracts by the Author of The Cloud of Unknowing.* SLG Press, 1982.

_____ *The Book of Privy Counseling* in W. Johnson, trans. *The Cloud of Unknowing and the Book of Privy Counseling.* Image, 1973.

## ARTICLES

Ashley, Benedict. "St. Catherine of Siena's Principles of Spiritual Direction," *Spirituality Today*, 33 (1981) 43-52.

Asselin, David. "Christian Maturity and Spiritual Discernment," *Review for Religious*, 27 (1968) 581-595.

Brockman, Norbert. "Spiritual Direction: Training and Charism," *Sisters Today*, 48 (1976) 104-109.

Carlson, Gregory. "Spiritual Direction and the Paschal Mystery," *Review for Religious*, 33 (1974) 532-541.

Culligan, Kevin. "Towards a Contemporary Model of Spiritual Direction: A Comparative Study of St. John of the Cross and Carl Rodgers," *Carmelite Studies*, vol. 2. ICS Publications, 1982, pp. 95-166.

Dominic, Paul. "A Biblical Image of the Retreat Director," *Review for Religious*, 35 (1976) 279-282.

Frison, Basil. "Spiritual Direction as an Opening to the Experience of God," *Contemplative Review*, 13 (2, 1980) 20-26.

Gaffney, James. "An Unpublished Treatise of Augustine Baker on Discernment," *American Benedictine Review*, 25 (1974) 235-245.

Geromel, Eugene. "Depth Psychotherapy and Spiritual Direction," *Review for Religious*, 36 (1977) 753-763.

Giallanza, Joel. "Integration in Spiritual Direction," *Contemplative Reivew*, 13 (4, 1980) 31-39.

Giallanza, Joel. "Spiritual Direction According to St. John of the Cross," *Contemplative Review*, 11 (3, 1978) 31-37.

Giallanza, Joel. "Spiritual Direction According to St. Teresa of Avila," *Contemplative Review*, 12 (2, 1979) 1-9.

Grady, Laureen. "Afterword to a Pistle of Discrecioun of Stirings," *Contemplative Review*, 10 (2, 1977) 1-6.

Healey, Charles. "Thomas Merton: Spiritual Director," *Cistercian Studies*, 11 (3, 1976) 228-245.

Kilduff, Thomas. "Spiritual Direction and Personality Types," *Spiritual Life*, 26 (3, 1980) 149-158.

Lienhard, Joseph. "On Discernment of Spirits in the Early Church," *Theological Studies*, 41 (1980) 505-529.

Sheets, John. "Profile of the Spirit: A Theology of Discernment of Spirits," *Review for Religious*, 30 (1971) 363-376.

Sweeney, Richard. "Discernment in the Spiritual Direction of St. Francis de Sales," *Review for Religious*, 39 (1980) 127-141.

Walsh, William. "Reality Therapy and Spiritual Direction," *Review for Religious*, 35 (1976) 372-385.

Ware, Kallistos. "The Spiritual Father in Orthodox Christianity," *Cross Currents*, 24 (1974) 296-313.